DENNIS KING

THE DAILY B'ALMANAC

TIPS AND WISDOM
FOR THE SERIOUS BASKETBALL PLAYER

outskirts
press

"I looked up at the scoreboard and thought, Has there ever been a boy who loved this game as much as I have loved it? I had known the praise of crowds and knew nothing else on earth to equal it. When I played basketball, I was possessed by a nakedness of spirit, an absolute purity, a divine madness when I was let loose to ramble between the lines."

Pat Conroy
From *THE LORDS OF DISCIPLINE*

COVER PHOTO: 2013 Tennessee State Quarter Finals – Asa Duvall's *"The Shot Heard 'Round the State"* rips through the nets as Brentwood High School upsets #1 ranked and 30-0 Blackman High School 52-49. Andrew Collignon Photography 2013

AUTHOR'S NOTE: The range of entries for THE DAILY B'ALMANAC covers a six-month period starting on October 15th and ending on April 15th. The first date corresponds with the official start of basketball season for a majority of state high school associations. The second date aligns with the approximate end of the NCAA college basketball playoffs.

OTHER BOOKS WRITTEN BY DENNIS KING

REFUSE TO BE ORDINARY: 10 Championship Traits (2012)
WE BALL Y'ALL: Diary of a Championship Quest (2014)
THE ART OF BASKETBALL WAR by Moon Tzu (pseudonym) (2017)
All available at *AMAZON.COM* or *OUTSKIRTSPRESS.COM*

ACKNOWLEDGEMENT

The author would like to acknowledge former standout guard John Smithheisler (Brentwood High Class of 2000) for his extensive input and contributions to this project. John's astute observations, insights and basketball I.Q. were invaluable during the entire process.

A special thank you to Steven Flook for researching the birthdays of NBA and WNBA players, coaches and Hall-of-Famers.

This book is dedicated to the beautiful,
but brief lives of former students and players:

DONNY CAROTHERS

FRANKIE BUKOVAC

SCOTT HARTMAN

BEN DOUGHERTY

KRISTEN LYELL

KURT RIESSLER

WILLIE HOGUE

BRIAN FOX

JASON LAWING

ABE GRAHAM

CURT WILLIAMS

MIKE MORAN

SAM HALL

MICHAEL OVERCASH

MITCH SPAULDING

KIMMY JONES

SAM McGAHREN

BLAKE ESHENRODER

JOHN MILLER

INTRODUCTION

This book is for serious players only. The window is tiny. The season of youth is brief. For your athletic talent to fully blossom, the seeds of hunger must fall on fertile soil at a very critical time in your life.

Dedicated basketball players must learn to "think the game." Adding a cerebral component to your preparation and development provides the winner's edge. THE DAILY B'ALMANAC is designed to provide mental nourishment, offer a daily vitamin for each day of basketball season and administer a booster shot of insight and reflection.

This book is a compendium of basketball knowledge and life skills written specifically for the millions of serious young basketball players worldwide. More importantly, it provides strategies and language for sensitive issues that arise in every young athlete's life and is designed to help him or her navigate through the confusion of adolescence. Many of these topics have never been addressed with the concise honesty offered in this book and frankly, could be applied at any level of competition.

The DAILY B'ALMANAC provides instruction, insight, tips and wisdom. The range of the book encompasses the six-month period of official basketball season from October 15 to April 15. Each page includes famous birthdays, an instructional entry, an inspirational sports quote gleaned from *Twitter* feeds and an occasional *YouTube* link where appropriate. These *YouTube* links provide a second layer of interactive learning that reinforce the lessons with compelling visuals.

There is no greater classroom than the arena of competitive sports. These contrived exhibitions of 'skill and will' define and deepen self-understanding, cultivate the joy of teamwork and help to produce the most important ingredient for success in any life endeavor which experts now simply call - GRIT.

Good luck on your journey and remember to "scan the entire court."

OCTOBER 15

BIRTHDAY: Aaron Affalo 85, Jakob Poeltl 95

DREAMS

Dreams power the universe. The seed of a dream mysteriously takes root, but once it fastens inside the human mind, it is nearly impossible to remove. A budding young basketball player must create an internal and external environment of positive dream reinforcement. Surround yourself with dream-sharers, soak up knowledge from older mentors, and study the game with inquisitive eyes. Dreams fuel action and when they ignite they can blaze a path to greatness. Every great champion lived alone with his dreams long before he/she stood on a podium or raised a trophy.

TWITTER WISDOM: "Don't wait for your ship to come in. Row out to meet it." - @hinesight

OCTOBER 16

BIRTHDAY: Sue Bird 80, Manute Bol 62, *Dave Debusshere 40

OFFENSIVE REBOUNDING

Great offensive rebounders possess three traits: anticipation, technique and a mindset of relentless pursuit. Through the years only a few players like Moses Malone, Dennis Rodman, Tristan Thompson, Kenneth Faried and Yolanda Griffith have distinguished themselves with this talent. These players assume that every shot is actually a pass to themselves. The first objective is to read the trajectory, spin and distance of the shot. Anticipating where the ball will career off the rim provides a distinct advantage. Simultaneously, one must avoid being boxed out by knifing past the defender, spinning immediately upon contact or swim stroking the raised arm of the person boxing out (pushing down on the opponents arm in a swimming motion). Finally, a tenacious determination to pursue the rebound can result in some crucial second shots. You may not always retrieve the basketball, but if you get a hand on it, tap it backwards and keep it alive by your effort, the ball might fall into the hands of a teammate. Coaches love players who are relentless offensive rebounders.

TWITTER WISDOM: "Hustle beats muscle when muscle doesn't hustle." – Jon Gordon

YOUTUBE ASSIST – Elite Offensive Rebounding Big Men: Quick Hitters – "BballBreakdown" 3:27

OCTOBER 17

BIRTHDAY: Danny Ferry 66, Steve "Snapper" Jones 42

GETTING OPEN ON THE WING

Getting open on the wing requires some strategy. Some tenacious defenders make it their mission to deny you the ball. You must create a clear window for a successful pass. Many players try to get open by aimlessly darting out and back toward the sideline without any purpose. A three step process can generally free you to receive the ball - **STEP IN, SLIDE UP, POP OUT.** 1. Walk your player slowly toward the lane and step into his crotch area while making some light contact with your forearm to his chest. 2. Slide vertically up the lane a step or two. 3. Pop out at a flat 180 degree angle toward the sideline. This technique requires some practice, but it is highly effective.

TWITTER WISDOM: "The best players want excellence demanded of them." Mike Krzyzewski

YOUTUBE ASSIST - Ways to Get Open Without the Basketball: "Championship Productions" 3:26

OCTOBER 18

BIRTHDAY: Brittney Griner 90, Terry Furlow 54, John Johnson 47

ESCAPING A SHOOTING SLUMP

Slumps occur to every athlete in every sport. Any competitive skill that requires precision and finesse is subject to mysterious miscalculations of the brain whether it's putting a golf ball, hitting a baseball or shooting a basketball. The first step in recovery is to consciously acknowledge that the slump phenomenon is universal. Do not internalize or personalize the 'slump' because that will simply increase the pressure and frustration. Remember, you WILL return to normalcy once your mechanics and mindset slide back into synch. Some successful techniques that have worked for elite basketball players through the years are rather simple: 1. Shoot with your opposite hand for a half an hour. When you return to shooting with your natural hand the brain might 'reset' on its own. 2. Get a bit more thrust on the jump of your jump shot. This permits a split-second longer for target adjustment. 3. Change environments- do something you haven't done in a while (movie, listen to music you use to love, visit an old friend from elementary school, walk in the woods, play another sport). This will activate different parts of your brain and release pressure.

TWITTER WISDOM: "Everybody has the same amount of time during the day. You can either spend your time or invest it." – Chip Kelly

YOUTUBE ASSIST – 3 Reasons your shot is broke: Basketball Shooting, "ShotMechanics" 6:40

OCTOBER 19

BIRTHDAY: Brad Daugherty 65, Joe 'Jelly Bean' Bryant 54, Lionel Hollins 53

EYE CONTACT

"The eyes are the windows to the soul" is a famous quote. You can see fear in a person's eyes. You can tell if someone is lying by staring into their eyes. You can see determination and fire in a person's eyes. The eyes of human beings are wonderful instruments of communication. When a coach or teacher provides instruction for your personal growth, the most respectful thing you can do is look them in the eyes. You are signaling to them that they have your full attention. Players should "listen with their eyes" in every huddle. Looking at the floor, or gazing into the crowd demonstrates a lack of focus and engagement. Direct eye contact and a quick nod of understanding send an encouraging sign that you are fully present and absorbing the coach's message.

TWITTER WISDOM: "Athlete - you are a billboard for your school, your team, your family, your parents, your coach and everyone who has worn the uniform." @proactivecoach

OCTOBER 20

BIRTHDAY: Rodney Hood 92, Eddie Jones 71, Taj McWilliams 70

UNIQUE WEAK HAND DRILLS

Button your shirt with your weak hand, eat with your weak hand, text with your weak hand, write with your weak hand, zip your fly with your weak hand, learn to juggle. Train the brain to become comfortable with the uncomfortable. Change your foul shot routine to include a couple of weak hand bounces every time you practice – you'll get 10,000 more repetitions with your weak hand. In addition there are hundreds of youtube instruction videos that involve cones, two ball dribbling, dribbling off the wall, doing sit-ups while slamming the ball between your legs, using different size balls – tennis balls, volleyballs, BIG BALLS; dribbling between and around your legs, around the back, inside out, push-pulls, hard slams, cross-overs, machine gun two-hand patter and much more. Go hard enough to make mistakes and chase the ball. Become a dribbling virtuoso with amazing dexterity.

TWITTER WISDOM: "One moment, one step, one day at a time. Fall in love with the Journey/Process!" Deshaun Watson

YOUTUBE ASSIST -5 Minutes To SICK Handles with Coach Drew Hanlen: "EGT Basketball" 4:44

OCTOBER 21

BIRTHDAY: Damion Lee 92, Ricky Rubio 90, *Vern Mikkelsen 28

GRATITUDE

When a teammate delivers a perfect pass to you for a layup, make sure you acknowledge him or her with a quick finger point. When a teammate dives on the floor to recover a loose ball or sacrifices his body to take a charge, rush over and help him/her up from the floor. Showing gratitude is a selfless gesture that strengthens the ties of brother/sisterhood. There is a song lyric that states, "The next best thing to playing and winning is playing and losing." We have all heard that competitors are supposed to hate to lose, but the songwriter recognizes that there is dignity and honor in just competing. One should be grateful just for the chance to play a sport. There are many whose physical challenges have prevented them from ever experiencing the exhilaration of competition.

TWITTER WISDOM: "When's the last time you have made known to someone else by words or actions how grateful you are for the deposit they made in your life?" - #3DCoaching

OCTOBER 22

BIRTHDAY: Brad Stevens 76, *Drazen Petrovich 64, *Slater Martin 25

GOOD SHOT-BAD SHOT

A bad shot is the first pass that starts an opponent's fast break. The score and the time on the clock must always dictate what kind of shot, where it is taken, and who is taking it. During the flow of any game, a good shot is one that has a chance of being rebounded by the offense. But there are times down the stretch when the team with a lead must work for layups only. When a team is behind, the tendency is to cast up long 3's off the dribble instead of making one extra pass or penetrating to kick for a shot taken in rhythm. Also, a quick '2' should never be overlooked. There are also times when a shot is taken much too early in the possession, and there are times when the wrong person decides to shoot. Coaches cringe when players invent shots they've never practiced by wiggling and contorting just to get the ball to the rim. These low percentage shots might please the unwashed masses in the stands, but they actually sabotage victory.

TWITTER WISDOM: "I don't care about the result, I just care that we have no regrets. The pain of discipline isn't as bad as the pain of regret." –Brad Stevens

YOUTUBE ASSIST - Winning with Shot Selection | PGC Basketball, "PGC Basketball" 4:12

OCTOBER 23

BIRTHDAY: Tayler Hill 90, Jordan Crawford 88, Keith Van Horn 75

SHOOTING FORM –
ONE SIZE DOES NOT FIT ALL

There is nothing prettier or more aesthetically pleasing than watching a classic jump shot – the lift with slight forward momentum, the elbow rising tight near the body, the ball nestled softly on the pads of the fingers, the rainbow arc of an orange rotating sphere, the frozen follow through of a bent wrist and the splash into netted twine. This shooting motion is not easily replicated for a number of reasons, but the most obvious is physiology. Our skeletal and muscular frameworks are all different. Our appendages are attached with different soft-tissue properties. Our joints have different flexibility issues. Arm length, hand size and eye dominance all figure into the equation. Despite all of the instruction on shooting mechanics, our jump shots are like fingerprints. Everyone's is slightly different. Our physiology ultimately dictates our shooting form, and after years of repetitive shooting drills, a young player gravitates to a shooting form that seems to work best for him/her. Yes, tweaks to one's form might produce minimal improvement, but there will always be players with unconventional releases that are lethal shooters.

TWITTER WISDOM: "There are two things you can do – prove them right or prove them wrong." – Julian Edelman

YOUTUBE ASSIST: How to find YOUR perfect shooting form: Basketball shooting Tips and Tricks – "ShotMechanics" 7:35

OCTOBER 24

BIRTHDAY: Jaylen Brown 96, Nicola Vucevic 90

DEFENSIVE ANTICIPATION

What secrets do the great defenders possess? Why are some players dangerously disruptive on defense? Why are some players considered "ball-hawks" who deflect and steal passes out of mid-air? Yes, these players are probably very quick and have great reaction time, but they also possess the intangible instinct of anticipation. Anticipation involves a form of seeing into the future. By reading the eyes of the passer, by calculating the time and distance of a pass, by cheating or hedging in a certain direction and by gambling on a predictable passing angle, a ball hawk can create havoc. A sense of anticipation increases with experience. The more times a player observes specific situations, the more he/she can predict how the play will unfold.

TWITTER WISDOM: "The more thorough, the more extensive, the more rehearsed, the better you perform under the pressure of any situation that calls for an immediate decision." – Bill Walsh

YOUTUBE ASSIST - Kawhi Leonard Defense : Lockdown How To, "Coach Mike" 4:51

OCTOBER 25

BIRTHDAY: Chandler Parsons 88, *Dave Cowens 48, Dan Issel 48, *Zelmo Beatty 39

CONFRONTING A TEAMMATE

In an ideal world, all players love and respect their teammates, understand and embrace their role on the team, and never allow jealousy or resentment to enter their minds. Many teams aspire to this ideal, but upon rare occasion, a teammate's behavior and attitude can sometimes become intolerable. Team morale and performance begin to suffer and confrontation becomes unavoidable. There is really no golden strategy because every situation carries its own special circumstances, but there are some general rules to follow. 1. Address the issue directly with the person in a non-threatening environment appealing to their sense of team. Simply ask them if they are aware of how the team seems to be affected by their behavior or attitude? Do not use an accusatory tone and be sure to listen attentively. Expect some defensiveness, but do not allow the verbal volume to escalate. Merely calling attention to the problem can sometimes help. 2. In a team setting, reinforce the collective goals and expectations that everyone agrees to follow. Clarification of values and a show of unity can be effective. 3. Confide the problem to a coach. Coaches are sometimes oblivious to the social dynamics of their team. The coach may determine that intervention is necessary, or maybe provide a different insight or perspective that had not been considered.

TWITTER WISDOM: "Great teammates don't protect each other when someone's out of line. They protect the culture. No one is bigger than the team." – Bob Shipley

OCTOBER 26

BIRTHDAY: Monta Ellis 85, Nick Collison 80, Hot Rod Hundley 34, *Joe Fulks 21

LEADING THE FAST-BREAK

Running the fast-break is a numbers game. The ball-handler must make critical split-second decisions to be successful. If the break is 2 on 1, the ball-handler should declare a side and drive to the hoop to draw the defender to him/her. This allows for a simple assist. If the break is a 3 on 1, the dribbler must dribble directly at the defender to freeze him in place thus opening up both wing passing lanes. If the break is a 3 on 2 the quickest score is a pass to the wing and back to the point, or a pass to the wing and a quick pass to the opposite wing cutting to the ball-side block. After delivering the pass, the ball-handler must always veer or jump-stop to avoid the charge. Sometimes there are gray areas in which the fast-break is not attacking a clean configuration because the retreating players may be challenging further out. The ball-handler might now have to deliver the pass earlier and at a sharper angle. He might also have to maintain his dribble, flair to the wing and look for trailers diving down the lane.

TWITTER WISDOM: "DYK sleep loss severely decreases your ability to create memories and your reaction time? Shoot for 8-10hrs of sleep every night to be on an elite level mentally and physically." - Sidney Smith

OCTOBER 27

BIRTHDAY: Lonzo Ball 97, Evan Turner 88, Andrew Bynum 87, Crystal Langhorne 86, Lou Williams 86

FINISHING THE FAST-BREAK

Catching the ball in full stride and sweeping in to finish a fast break is a beautiful sight, but a great finisher pays attention to three things: 1. Staying wide in his lane before planting his outside foot to angle sharply to the hoop. 2. Catching the ball with his eyes. Too often an imperfect pass is fumbled because the receiver looked at the rim too soon. 3. Anticipating contact with a defender and finishing through the contact with laser concentration. Do not allow being bumped while you are in the air affect where you place the ball on the backboard.

TWITTER WISDOM: "Little things make the difference. Everyone is well prepared in the big things, but only the winners perfect the little things." – Bear Bryant

YOUTUBE ASSIST – How to Finish Layups Over Taller Defenders: Basketball Moves for Shorter Players: "Shot Mechanics" 4:04

OCTOBER 28

BIRTHDAY: Andrew and Aaron Harrison 94, Jarrett Jack 83, *Lenny Wilkins 37, Butch van Breda Kolff 22

FAILURE

Winston Churchill once said, "Success is never final, and failure is never fatal." There are a thousand other clichés and quotes that discuss the psychology of failure, and how humans should respond to setbacks. The simplest wisdom regarding failure is this – every single person has the power within to control his/her response to any setback no matter how great or small. You choose the interpretation. Will the event have a permanent negative impact or will it produce positive motivation? Will you be crushed or inspired? Will you be a victim or a tougher, wiser human being? Michael Jordan said it best: "I've missed more than 9000 shots in my career. I've lost almost 300 games. Twenty-six times, I've been trusted to take the game winning shot and missed. I've failed over and over and over again in my life. And that is why I succeed."

TWITTER WISDOM: "Giving up is the greatest failure." – Unknown

YOUTUBE ASSIST - Failure | Basketball Motivation Video, "DEVO Highlights Presents" 10:12

OCTOBER 29

BIRTHDAY: Evan Fournier 92, Dick Garmaker 32

SPACING

Spacing is a critical component for successful offensive play. When players are properly spaced, every "set"play has a better chance of being successful. Spacing also contributes dramatically to the success of any motion offense or press-breaker as well. Proper spacing creates more room to operate because defensive players must travel farther to provide help. Proper spacing also allows more space to complete a give-and-go, a pick-and-roll, a dribble-drive, a penetrate and kick, a post-feed and kick-out or a 1-on-1 clear out. Many players contribute to a sluggish offense because they neglect to pay attention to the precise distances prescribed by the design of the offense.

TWITTER WISDOM: "No one has ever drowned in sweat." – Lou Holtz

OCTOBER 30

BIRTHDAY: Devin Booker 96, Phil Chenier 50, Glen Combs 46

GUARDING A SIZE MISMATCH

Occasionally, a defensive switch will occur in which a smaller guard ends up defending a larger post player in the paint. The conventional wisdom is that the offense should immediately take advantage of the mismatch and force the ball inside for an easy score. Executing this strategy sounds much easier than it really is. If a smaller guard refuses to be posted up and fights to get in front of the larger player, the passing target is reduced to a pinpoint lob. If there is some alert off-side help already in position, the pass is now a risky option. Add some serious ball-pressure on the passer, and the strategy is completely thwarted. The key for success, however, rests mainly with the smaller guard recognizing the danger and urgently battling to front the larger man.

TWITTER WISDOM: "Toughness is a talent. I would take true toughness over talent every day." - Jay Bilas

YOUTUBE ASSIST – How Good was 5 foot 3 Muggsy Bogues? "NBAGotGameTV" 10:28

OCTOBER 31

BIRTHDAY: Antonio Davis 68, Blue Edwards 65, John Lucas 53, Luke Jackson 41

SIMPLIFY, SIMPLIFY, SIMPLIFY

"Simplify, simplify, simplify." Nearly two hundred years ago, philosopher Henry David Thoreau pronounced this recommendation to the world. Imagine what his reaction would be to our cluttered, crazy, complex world today. This same principle should be applied to developing your skills. A wise tennis coach instructed his pupil who wanted to experiment with a variety of shots, "Just hit the same old boring winner." Master a few "go-to" moves – for a post-player it might be a drop-step power move, a windmill step-through, a baby-hook, or an elbow jumper. For a guard it might be a great change-of-pace, a killer-crossover, or catching and shooting without a dribble. Hit the same boring winner.

TWITTER WISDOM: I fear not the man who has practiced 10,000 kicks once. I fear the man who has practiced one kick 10,000 times." - Bruce Lee

NOVEMBER 1

BIRTHDAY: Tim Frazier 90, Eric Spoelstra 70, Jumpin' Joe Caldwell 42

---

10 TIPS FOR MAKING THE TEAM

1. Play as much pick-up ball with current team members as you can. One good word from a player will open a coach's eyes.
2. If possible, be part of the pre-season conditioning program.
3. Go to tryouts in shape.
4. Be early and make sure all forms have been filled out.
5. Wear a distinctive or colorful t-shirt or shorts.
6. Don't be timid. Volunteer to play defense when the coach needs players, be the first in line for drills.
7. Be vocal and encourage others when they make a good play.
8. Do every drill with total hustle.
9. Ask questions of returning players if you don't understand directions.
10. If you get cut, at the appropriate time consider asking the coach to come to one of your YMCA or REC League games to see you play in person. Many coaches will accept the invitation

TWITTER WISDOM: Courage doesn't always roar. Sometimes courage is a little voice at the end of the day that says, 'I'll try again tomorrow.' –Mary Radmacher

YOUTUBE ASSIST -Top 6 Tryout Hacks: How to Make the Basketball Team - "ShotMechanics" 8:07.

NOVEMBER 2

BIRTHDAY: Keith Jennings 68, Ron Lee 52

SLIPPING SCREENS

Slipping a screen is an effective counter to teams that predictably hedge high or switch ball screens. Instead of the screener coming to a jump stop, splitting the ball-defender's leg with a wide stance and bracing for impact, the screen-slipper gives every indication of setting the screen but at the last second plants and blasts toward the hoop at a sharp angle hoping for an alert pass. The slip is effective because it surprises the two defenders who are expecting a conventional pick and roll and may be momentarily confused in their defensive roles. When two offensive players develop some chemistry, they can sense each other's instinct for this maneuver.

TWITTER WISDOM: "Your value doesn't decrease based on some-one's inability to see your worth. " – Bob Holden

YOUTUBE ASSIST – "Slip Screen Plays, "Michael Thompson" 3:01

NOVEMBER 3

BIRTHDAY: Ty Lawson 87, Tyler Hansbrough 85, *George Yardley 28

SHOT BLOCKING

Shot blocking is an art. Some players simply have the timing, reflexes and arm length to swat shots, however, there are actually some techniques that can be learned. Great shot blockers always maintain a tiny bit of space between bodies. When an offensive player cannot feel contact, he/she is out in space and rarely can draw a foul. Secondly, the shot blocker should already have his blocking arm raised and poised so that the block is a mere wrist flick. Thirdly, the best place to block the ball is when it is a few inches away from the shooter's hand. This allows for some control of where the ball lands. Big impressive bleacher-swats are pointless because the opponent regains possession. Finally, do not swat downward in a large sweeping motion that might catch the shooter on his arms or shoulder. Don't make the referee's job easy.

TWITTER WISDOM: "I'm not looking for the best players, I'm looking for the right ones." – Herb Brooks

YOUTUBE ASSIST – How to Block Shots: Blocking Shots the SMART Way! "Shot Science Basketball" 3:50

NOVEMBER 4

BIRTHDAY: Lorenzon Wright 75, Dick Groat 30

SCREAMING COACHES

A lot of coaches scream. Sports are competitive and emotional. It is important to always filter out the content from the tone. Coaches in general, love the game and love to teach and work with young athletes in a competitive atmosphere. They want to teach them about life and the lessons that arise from winning, losing, teamwork and sportsmanship. A message that is delivered harshly, naturally triggers a defensive reaction, but try to be resilient and receptive to the message. Exposure to all coaching styles prepares you for a variety of communication strategies encountered in life. Don't shrink and don't take it personally. Be stoic, learn and grow.

TWITTER WISDOM: "You can't shut down. There's going to be adversity in the game that's way tougher than your coach yelling at you." – Ryan Keith Russell

YOUTUBE ASSIST - What If Your Coach Yells At You | PGC Basketball | Mental Toughness, "PGC Basketball" 4:52

NOVEMBER 5

BIRTHDAY: Trey Lyles 95, O.J. Mayo 87, Jerry Stackhouse 74, *Bill Walton 52

FOUL SHOT RECOVERY

Regaining possession of the ball after a missed foul shot is always a sweet bonus, but sometimes it can swing momentum or even win a game. There are some standard and advanced strategies that create block out problems for the opponent. The first technique is the CUP AND SLASH. Since the offense must line up in the second box on the lane, the first offensive rebounder will make contact with the man blocking him out, then spin (CUP) to the outside toward the baseline fighting to gain position in front of the man blocking him out. The block out man will be occupied and forced to push out further than comfortable leaving some space under his side of the hoop. Simultaneously, the opposite offensive rebounder SLASHES across the lane into that small vacated space. He must out-quick the man trying to block him out. If the first shot is successful, the offensive players can flip-flop assignments and execute the same strategy from the opposite side in mirror image. Some other individual tips involve starting higher in the box to create more distance from the man trying to block you out, turning your body to face the baseline like a sprinter to make you quicker and more unpredictable, or if you are larger and stronger raise your arms above your head and simply BULLDOZE the opponent under the net where the opponent's rebounding range is severely reduced.

TWITTER WISDOM: "Pressure can bust pipes or make diamonds." – Tim S. Grover

NOVEMBER 6

BIRTHDAY: Lamar Odom 79, Phog Allen 1885

RESPECT

Respect has wide and various meanings. In basketball you earn respect by effort, attitude and results. It is easy to despise an opponent whose defensive pressure harasses you all over the floor, but you secretly respect his tenacity. It's easy to hate a player who taunts you when you get knocked down, but you respect the player who reaches out a hand to help you up. It is easy to resent the player who burned your team for 30 points, but you've got to respect the talent and hours of sweat that produced his/her efficiency. The bottom line is that we respect people who consistently hold themselves to the highest standards of effort, behavior and decency.

TWITTER WISDOM: "There are two ways to do something. The right way, and again." - #NavySEALS

NOVEMBER 7

BIRTHDAY: Tony Jackson 42, Al Attles 36

GUARDING A SUPERSTAR

If you are chosen to guard a great offensive player consider it a rare opportunity. So many players shrink from this challenge because they are not true competitors. They are afraid of public embarrassment and would rather hide in anonymity. Great competitors request the assignment. Great competitors are flattered when they receive the assignment. Great competitors focus on the mission of simply slowing down the scorer, not shutting down the scorer. In reality, it requires a team strategy to limit a superstar's effectiveness. The first step is to tenaciously deny the ball to the superstar and defend in "no-help" mode. When transitioning to defense, find and sprint to the superstar as quickly as is prudent. Doing this might limit his/her transition points. Secondly, when he/she receives the ball, the defender should do one of two things - dictate the direction of the first dribble (preferably to their weak hand), or sink and sag if the superstar's strength is more penetration than shooting (this sometimes results in the superstar passing more). Thirdly, teammates must be willing to give early help by cheating towards the ball or hedging high on ball screens. Finally do not foul and put the superstar to the line for free shots. Holding a superstar under his/her average is a moral victory.

TWITTER WISDOM: "Warriors take chances. Like everyone else, they fear failing. But they refuse to let fear control them." – Samurai Proverb

YOUTUBE ASSIST - Lockdown Defense | Skills Training | "PGC Basketball" 7:52

Shutting Down A Star Player | Skills Training | "PGC Basketball" 5:26

NOVEMBER 8

BIRTHDAY: Brevin Knight 75, *Tom 'Satch' Sanders 38, Frank McGuire 13

UNPLUG

Young people are bombarded constantly by competing social pressures - television, social media, billboards, demanding coaches, academic expectations, cliques, peer pressure, deadlines and part-time jobs. Sometimes it is important to just TURN DOWN THE NOISE. A person touches his/her phone 2,617 times a day for phone calls, texts, email, social media, internet, streaming, video games and the list goes on. By occasionally unplugging from our digital slave-masters, we can de-clutter our brains and focus on our priorities of self-growth. It will be difficult at first, but try to make it a ritual of unplugging for periods of time. You will be re-booting your genuine, true and natural connection to the world.

TWITTER WISDOM: "Eliminate the clutter and all the things that are going on outside and focus on the things that you can control." – Nick Saban

NOVEMBER 9

BIRTHDAY: *Frank Selvy 32

TRAPPING

Trapping an offensive player is a defensive gamble. If done properly, it can lead to valuable turnovers. If done sloppily, it can lead to easy scores by the opponent. There are places on the basketball floor that can be considered 'tar-pits', those dangerous ancient bogs where prehistoric animals got stuck and perished. All four corners of the half-court are 'tar-pits'. When an offensive player is funneled into one of these spots, two attacking trappers should do the following: 1. Quickly clamp the trap, closing off the two escape routes. 2. Ideally, try to have the inside feet of the two trappers touch. 3. The inside arm of one trapper should be high, the inside arm of the other trapper should be lower. This helps to prevent the offensive player from splitting the trap with his head or ball. 4. Loud vocalization of the word "DEAD" can unnerve the offensive player.

If the trap arrives late, the two trappers must corral the dribbler. Do not allow the dribbler to split the trap or drive sideline/baseline. Both trappers must move their feet to cut- off the dribbler hoping to make him/her pick up the ball. Another effective trapping angle in the half court is for the man guarding the ball-handler to follow the first pass and trap an unsuspecting dribbler who is preoccupied with his own defender. This might be particularly effective if the dribbler is angling down the sideline.

TWITTER WISDOM: "Success isn't owned it is leased, and rent is due every day. . . If you're not consistently improving someone else is. Every single practice I treat like a game." - J.J. Watt

YOUTUBE ASSIST - Shaka Smart 1-2-1-1 Havoc full court press, "CoachBase" 5:38

NOVEMBER 10

BIRTHDAY: Tony Snell 91, D.J. Augustin 87, Kendrick Perkins 84, John Williamson 51,

WARM-UP RITUALS

Preparing to play is a vital component of consistent performance. Develop a conscious routine that not only warms and activates muscle groups, but also channels the mind into maximum focus. On game day many players choose to synchronize naps with visualization, personal music and a standard pre-game menu. At the gym, serious players participate in personal rituals of stretching, ball handling and slow-motion shooting progressions before they even step onto the floor. Once on the floor, do not neglect rehearsing some defensive slides because half of the game is played with a different set of muscles. Players should "groove" their shot by starting close to the basket and slowly working their way outward concentrating on precise shooting form. Finally, begin to take game speed shots from spots where you will most likely get open.

TWITTER WISDOM: "Basketball isn't just a sport, it is an art - one that must be mastered to succeed." – Steph Curry

YOUTUBE ASSIST: 5 Shooting Drills For GAME DAY with Coach Damin Altizer, "EGTbasketball" 7:40

NOVEMBER 11

BIRTHDAY: Rudy Larusso 37

SHORT MEMORY AFTER A MISTAKE

If you run over a squirrel don't look in the rearview mirror because around the bend there might be a moose standing in the middle of the road. Your bad pass, bad shot or stupid foul cannot be erased by pouting or feeling sorry for yourself. Move on. Do the next RIGHT THING RIGHT whether it's sprinting back on defense, communicating alertly to a teammate or being in proper defensive position. Blaming someone else, putting your head down or slowly jogging back hoping that everyone sees how disappointed you are is 'loser' behavior. Nobody has ever played a flawless game. Do not allow a mistake to linger or cloud your focus.

TWITTER WISDOM: "What to do with a mistake - • Recognize It • Admit It • Learn From It • Forget It" –Dean Smith

NOVEMBER 12

BIRTHDAY: Russell Westbrook 88, Corey Maggette 79

DON'T AGONIZE, ORGANIZE

You will be amazed what adding a little more organization to your life will do. Modern life can be cluttered with academic deadlines, responsibilities, expectations and family commitments that gobble up your time. Developing personal systems that reduce chaos and help you to maximize your time will bring untold benefits. Organize your room, closets and drawers - totally de-clutter. Living in a mess is simply juvenile rebellion. Start early in life writing things down in your phone or on a wall-calendar. Do NOT trust your memory. Plan your day the night before, and plan your week on Sunday night. Tackle large school projects in manageable increments. Starting earlier and knocking off small chunks requires some discipline, but you avoid the deadline monster that will swallow you whole. When you streamline your daily life, there is more quality time to pursue your basketball dreams.

TWITTER WISDOM: "Want to barely get by in life? Then barely get by in class, in workouts, with your chores, with your job, etc... Winning the lottery is not a plan." - Bob Shipley

NOVEMBER 13

BIRTHDAY: Shabazz Mohammed 92, Metta World Peace 79, Rollie Massimino 34

BOXING-OUT

Simply put, boxing-out is the concept of preventing an opponent from gaining a favorable rebounding position. Every defensive player has the responsibility to put a body on the person he is guarding. In the perfect 'box-out' scenario, a missed shot can actually land on the floor inside the middle of five defenders who have completely sealed off their opponent. When a shot is taken, some key techniques should be employed: 1. Quickly locate your man 2. Read his route to the basket 3. Make contact with an arm-bar then pivot to pin the opponent on your backside with a low base. 5. Release to retrieve the ball. Boxing-out while in a zone defense presents some unique problems because the defense is assigned *areas* instead of specific players. In an overloaded *area*, the defender must create some general contact then be "first" to the ball. Guards playing in a zone defense should always check the perimeter for crashing opponents then step into their path.

TWITTER WISDOM: "There is no substitution for hustle, and if you don't hustle there will be a substitution." – Tex Winter

YOUTUBE ASSIST – Boxing Out, "extremebballskills" 5:27

NOVEMBER 14

BIRTHDAY: Lionel Simmons 68, Jack Sikma 55, Simmie Hill 46

LOCKER ROOM POISON

The climate inside the locker room is important. The locker room is often an unsupervised social club that can strengthen team bonds, or foster dissension. There will always be pecking orders inside any group of human beings. Age, experience, knowledge, talent, physical maturity can all dictate some degree of status. A healthy locker room often rings with good-natured laughter and all players should feel comfortable inside this sanctuary. Occasionally, disgruntled players or selfishly immature players will abuse their membership on the team to voice personal criticism of coaches and other teammates. They may also team-up to bully, haze or demean younger players. NOTHING productive results from these actions. There is a void of leadership when this behavior occurs. Always be aware of the toxic elements that can slowly poison the locker room air.

TWITTER WISDOM: "Leaders must understand: silence is often a statement of acceptance." – Kevin Eastman

NOVEMBER 15

BIRTHDAY: Karl Anthony Townes 95, Bob Dandridge 47

BETTER CARDIO = HIGHER SCORING AVERAGE

"That player's got a lot of heart." This phrase often describes players who push themselves beyond the normal limits of hustle and exhaustion. Along with uncommon courage and discipline, players with big hearts generally have phenomenal cardio systems and literally do possess larger hearts. Basketball productivity unmistakably improves when your physical endurance is increased. A concerted off-season program designed to dramatically increase your cardio-vascular system will show results in the box score. Tired legs affect shooting form as well as the ability to finish contested layups late in games. Fatigue reduces winning the 50-50 loose balls or creating enough defensive pressure that could result in break-away steals and interceptions. Fatigue diminishes the chance of recovering an offensive rebound and powering it back into the hoop. Finally, fatigue will affect the speed needed to fill a fast-break lane that can result in an easy layup. Better cardio will get you more buckets.

TWITTER WISDOM: "Champions are built on a thousand invisible mornings." – Kirk Cousins

NOVEMBER 16

BIRTHDAY: Denzel Valentine 93, Amar'e Stoudemire 82, *Jo Jo White 46

HABITS

Your future success is hidden in your daily routine. Whether it is work-out habits, eating habits, practice habits, study habits, thought habits, sleep habits, listening habits or social habits, a young person is laying the foundation bricks for his/her effectiveness and productivity as an adult. At some point the ball won't bounce anymore. Although it is not an absolute one-to-one correlation, veteran teachers can often identify students who will become successful adults. Students who immediately take out his/her notebook or I-pad and begin to take notes, who turn in his/her work on time, and whose quality of work exceeds expectations are already fast-tracked for success. Most of these students do not have off-the-chart IQ's, they simply have adopted a discipline of habit that separate them from the pack.

TWITTER WISDOM: "Champions behave like champions before they're champions; they have a winning standard of performance before they're winners." – Bill Walsh

NOVEMBER 17

BIRTHDAY: Dragan Bender 97, *Elvin Hayes 45, Jim Boeheim 44

HOW TO TREAT REFEREES

Refereeing a sporting event is perhaps one of the most difficult jobs in the world. Fans can be absolutely irrational, and in some countries referees have actually been killed by irate, fanatical supporters. There is no doubt that there are varying degrees of proficiency throughout the ranks of officials in every sport, but players have an obligation to respect the men and women who make their game possible. Without officials hired to interpret and enforce the rules with split-second decisions, games become meaningless pick-up competitions. Keep your mouth shut when a foul is called on you. Hand or pass the ball respectfully to the nearest ref. Chase down an errant ball that trickles out of bounds as a favor to the ref. If you have a question or an issue that you need clarified, refer to the official as Mr. or Ms. Ref. There are no studies that suggest you will gain an advantage in later calls by behaving this way, but it certainly can't hurt. It also elevates the civility of the contest.

TWITTER WISDOM: "If character is what you do when no one is watching, then sportsmanship is what you do when everybody is watching." – Bob Ley

NOVEMBER 18

BIRTHDAY: Jason 'White Chocolate' Williams 75, Len Bias 63, Sam Cassell 69,

TAKING A CHARGE

The charge is the best play in basketball. It can wipe out a basket, add an additional personal and team foul to the opponent, make an aggressive player less confident and swing the emotional momentum of a game. Taking a charge is an art form. Of course it takes courage to sacrifice your body, but some players develop uncanny instincts to anticipate, bait and execute these contrived collisions with minimal discomfort. There are three keys: 1. Step up to meet the penetrator, plant a wide stationary base and protect your privates. 2. When contact is imminent, shift your weight to your heels and begin to fall slightly backward. 3. At the moment of contact, expel a loud grunt to alert the referee of the force of the impact, lift your head forward to keep it from hitting the floor, then slide on your butt and back to absorb the energy of hitting the floor. Sometimes a key opponent who is in serious foul trouble can be lured into a charge when he/she turns on a reverse dribble, cuts across the key toward the ball or makes a quick shoulder turn in the post.

TWITTER WISDOM: "Concentration leads to anticipation, which leads to recognition, which leads to execution, which leads to completion." – Bob Knight

YOUTUBE ASSIST - Dynamic Defense: How to Take a Charge in Basketball – "Better Basketball" 5:44

NOVEMBER 19

BIRTHDAY: Kenneth Faried 89, Andre Ingram 85

CONTRIBUTING FROM THE BENCH

Five are on the floor, but twelve are 'in' the game. Nothing disturbs a coach more than bench players who are not engaged. Players that slouch in their chairs, distract other bench-mates with immature behavior or try to interact with people in the crowd are sabotaging the mission of the team. During the course of a contest, a loud and supportive bench provides invaluable benefits. A great bench will warn teammates about blind-picks, back-doors or opponents who leak down court. A great bench will react to great hustle and momentum changing plays. A great bench will meet players coming off the floor at a time-out with enthusiasm and share observations that can help a teammate's performance. Staying engaged sends a clear message to your coach, that you are mentally primed to enter the game and contribute immediately.

TWITTER WISDOM: "A quiet bench is a losing bench, a quiet gym is a losing gym, and a quiet team is a losing team. Communicate and be enthusiastic!" – Bryce Tesdahl

NOVEMBER 20

BIRTHDAY: Carlos Boozer 81, Louie Dampier 44

IMPROVING YOUR GAME WHILE INJURED

Unfortunately, basketball players get injured. Being temporarily out-of-commission does not mean you can't improve. First of all, unless it is physically impossible, you should still attend every practice. Your presence sends a great message of support, and you develop a broader appreciation for the details of team preparation. You will view your teammates with a little different perspective when you are temporarily detached from competitive drills. Depending on the nature of your injury, there are countless ball-handling, passing and reflex drills that can be done while sitting in a chair. Get creative and perhaps recruit an assistant coach or a manager to help you complete the drills. If your foot is in a boot, you can still work on foul shots, short bank shots or some weak-hand dribbling and shooting. Maintaining your cardio poses the biggest problem when injured. Most injured players are able to do some limited weight lifting with either their legs or arms, ride a stationary bicycle or even swim laps in a swimming pool. When you are cleared to play, you can bring a new and improved game to the floor.

TWITTER WISDOM: "When you wake up, think about winning the day. Don't worry about a week or a month from now, just think about one day at a time." – Drew Brees

NOVEMBER 21

BIRTHDAY: Reggie Lewis 65, Cedric Maxwell 55, *Earl Monroe 44, Terry Dischinger 40

50–50 BALLS

Loose balls, contested rebounds, tipped dribbles and deflected passes occur in every game. Alert, quick and tenacious opportunists seem to end up with a higher percentage of successful recoveries. There is a mentality of competitiveness, hunger and willpower that seems to be the signature of certain programs. Perhaps the team adopts their coach's intensity by practicing every night with game speed urgency. Occasionally it comes down to players who are simply a different breed of dog. A rottweiler will get to a loose ball sooner than a poodle.

TWITTER WISDOM: "I don't care how big you are, how fast you are or who your daddy is. I care about how hard you play. Every play, every day. Be relentless." Bob Shipley

YOUTUBE ASSIST – Dave Cowens, "initialdma710" (start at 0.35 to 0:45)

NOVEMBER 22

BIRTHDAY: Benoit Benjamin 64, James Edwards 55

INFLUENCING A REFEREE'S CALL

All humans are susceptible to bias. This is why lawyers insist that the people they defend get haircuts, wear suits and are coached up on body language before they enter the court room. They don't want the jury to judge their clients based on pre-conceived biases. Although referees may intend to make every call fairly and correctly, they are humans. Players use a number of tricks to influence refs: loud grunts on block/charge calls, exaggerated head-lift when slightly bumped on a drive to the basket and quickly clapping and pointing in the direction of their basket on a disputed out-of-bounds call. These strategies may occasionally work, but the most effective tool is the long-game strategy of intentional respect. Courtesy, compliance, unemotional politeness when handing the ball to a ref can influence a referee to make a 50-50 call in your favor later in the game or later in the season when he/she is assigned to one of your more meaningful contests.

TWITTER WISDOM: "It is not all about talent. It's about dependability, consistency, being coachable, and understanding what you need to do to improve." – Bill Belichick

NOVEMBER 23

BIRTHDAY: Vin Baker 71, Steve Alford 64, Andrew Toney 57

DECEPTION AND MISDIRECTION

Every shot fake, jab step, V-cut, pass fake, slipped screen and back door cut is a LIE. You are purposely misleading the opponent in order to gain an advantage. Sports competition is one of the few places in society where being a good liar is admired.

Do NOT let your "fakes" look like "fakes". Overt gestures that exaggerate a shot or a pass, tip off the defender. There should be subtlety in your deception. A simultaneous torso lift and glance at the rim resembles a shooting motion far more than an exaggerated two-armed extension of the ball above your head. These rehearsed deceptions can make you a crafty and effective player. Fake with finesse.

TWITTER WISDOM: "You have a choice: You can throw in the towel or you can use it to wipe the sweat off your face." @coachmotto

NOVEMBER 24

SELF-INFLICTED PRESSURE

Relish the moment. Enjoy the opportunity to test your skill, will and courage, but don't put unnecessary pressure on yourself. The window of youth is brief. Beating yourself up for not meeting the expectations of yourself, parents, coaches or friends is counter-productive. In the big picture, individual games are forgettable events. Who won the 1960 World Series? In 1960 nearly every single citizen of the United States knew the answer. The Pittsburgh Pirates won the series in the bottom of the ninth inning in the seventh and final game. Today, virtually no one knows or cares. Sports are merely contrived competitions designed to provide energy outlets for the young, and amusement for the old. However, even though individual games may be quickly forgotten, sports do provide the most fertile training ground for character development, team dynamics and personal growth ever devised. When an athlete invests an inordinate amount of time, energy and emotion into a goal, he/she naturally feels a sense of pain and loss when that goal is thwarted, but a mature athlete knows that maintaining a balanced perspective is paramount. It is the journey not the destination that is important.

TWITTER WISDOM: "Pressure is a privilege." – Tim S. Grover

YOUTUBE ASSIST – How to Stop Being Nervous in Games Forever: "GetHandlesBasketball" 5:12

NOVEMBER 25

BIRTHDAY: Dennis Smith 97, Andrea Stinson 67, Lorenzo Charles 63

FOOTWORK

Pay attention to your footwork. Jump stops, pivots, defensive slides, spin dribbles, close-outs and post-ups all require coordination with your feet. Your feet provide the foundation that transfers your weight. Proper balance is necessary for effective execution. Quick changes of direction while sliding backwards are fundamentally unnatural movements since our knee joints are designed for forward walking. Drills that facilitate this skill can improve your all-around game. Football has always been ahead of the curve in footwork creativity. Running through tires, machine gun reaction drills, high-stepping through rope ladders, hopping over tackling dummies and two-footed stationary speed jumps are all designed to improve agility. Additional drills that address footwork include skipping rope, lane slides and pivoting around the 4-corners of the key. For some unconventional foot drills try some turbo hop-scotch, Irish step dancing or "dance, dance revolution."

TWITTER WISDOM: "Hard work doesn't have to be witnessed, time exposes EVERYTHING." – Susan Jackson

NOVEMBER 26

BIRTHDAY: Avery Bradley 90, Shawn Kemp 69

POST PLAY

An effective post player is worth his weight in uranium (more valuable than gold). When a team has a balanced inside and outside attack, they are very hard to defend. Great post players score in one of five ways: 1. Direct feed from the perimeter or high post. 2. Assist from a penetrator. 3. Offensive rebound. 4. In transition by beating their man down court. 5. Free throws.

Post players must DEMAND the ball with aggressive positioning. Step into the defender's body, pivot and show the passer your jersey numbers by raising your arms into goal posts. If the defender circles to the high side (toward foul line) push him higher, if he circles to the low side (toward baseline) push him lower. Keep your feet active and maintain a low, strong base. Be relentless and continue to re-post to create the best passing angle. As the game progresses, defenders begin to wear-down and the tough-minded post player will win the battle of wills. Experienced post players who are being effectively guarded will sometimes point to another spot or player on the floor (top of the key) who may have a better passing angle as they seal their defender on their back and only release when the ball is airborne. If the ball leads you to an easy shot, lay it in. If not, then once the ball is received, immediately secure it under the chin while assessing the pressure you feel on your body, or the pressure coming from other help defenders. A host of effective post moves can be employed including drop-step power moves, baby hooks, step-in windmills or turn-and-face live ball moves. The mindset of post-players should be to SCORE or GET FOULED. If these two goals are not being consistently achieved, guards will stop throwing the ball to you.

TWITTER WISDOM: "If you're good enough you're big enough." – Jay Bilas

YOUTUBE ASSIST – Post Moves Teaching Tape, "Ryan Krueger" 19:00

NOVEMBER 27

BIRTHDAY: Nick Van Exel 71, Jim Price 49

SCREENING

Screens are designed to impede, block and derail the smooth path of a defender. This can create scoring opportunities for a cutter or shooter. Effective screeners employ consistent techniques: 1. Signal with a raised fist to alert the ball-handler or cutter of your intention 2. Jump stop with a wide base and split the defender's closest leg 3. Expect contact and protect sensitive areas with your hands or arms 4. Hold your ground by shifting your weight slightly forward. Screens are part of every offense both man-to-man and zone. When a team precisely executes ball screens, down screens, back screens, cross screens and screen-ins, they dramatically increase the effectiveness of their offense. Savvy coaches will give significant playing time to players who excel at this fundamental skill even though their other abilities may be limited.

TWITTER WISDOM: "The minute you get away from fundamentals – proper technique, work ethic or mental prep – the bottom can fall out of your game." – Michael Jordan

YOUTUBE ASSIST – Monster Picks Set by 400 lb. High School Basketball Player, "Dennis King" 3:45

NOVEMBER 28

BIRTHDAY: Andrew Bogut 84, Leandro Barbosa 82, Roy Tarpley 64, Johnny Newman 63

PASSING WITH TOUCH

Touch, feel and finesse are words that describe the uncanny passing abilities that some players develop. Great passers have amazing anticipation and an understanding of velocity, trajectory and location in order to place the ball in a teammate's hands with pinpoint accuracy. For some people, this is simply a gift. They possess a superior modem in their brain that recognizes, decodes and computes with greater efficiency than average players. Others can develop 'touch' through trial and error. On the perimeter, players with touch always pass the ball away from the defender to prevent deflections. When feeding the post, they throw it to the shoulder furthest from the defender. On cross screens, the ball arrives almost simultaneously with the cutter. On fast breaks the ball leads the person sprinting in the lane so he/she doesn't have to break stride. On run-outs the ball is softly lofted so that the scorer can run under the ball with a direct line to the basket. On down screens the shooter receives the ball near his shooting pocket so he/she doesn't have to waste time adjusting the ball. There are no analytics that calculate a poorly thrown pass unless it results in a turnover. Sloppy, ill-timed or poorly located passes often go unnoticed. Precise, surgical passes delivered with 'touch' cannot be valued enough.

TWITTER WISDOM: "If you hate the coach who pushes you, who always says you have more to give and never lets you give anything than your absolute best? Wait 'til you play for a coach who doesn't care." - @CoachHinesCHS

YOUTUBE ASSIST – John Stockton: Passing Skills Compilation (Part 1), "TheCrunchySopa" 15:33

NOVEMBER 29

BIRTHDAY: Julius Randle 94, Jamal Mashburn 72, Dee Brown 68, George Thompson 47

DRIBBLING WITH PURPOSE

Dribble for these purposes only: 1. To advance the ball up the floor 2. To drive to the basket 3. To improve a passing angle 4. To attack a gap in a zone. Over-dribbling is a pointless and selfish exhibition that causes your teammates to stand around. Some players may have phenomenal handles, but unless they are being used expressly for the benefit of the team, negative things can happen. Unnecessary dribbling leads not only to team resentment, but can also lead to needless defeat. The untrained eye may be impressed with dexterous wizardry, but a seasoned veteran can spot a circus act from a mile away.

TWITTER WISDOM: "Adversity causes some men to break; others to break records." – William Arthur Ward

NOVEMBER 30

BIRTHDAY: Jordan Farmar 86, Natalie Williams, 70, Paul Westphal 50, Joe B. Hall 28

MY TURN TO SHOOT

Just because a shot goes in the basket does not mean it was a good shot. Just because you haven't taken a shot in a while, does not mean you should heave one up. The score, the time on the clock, the distance of the shot, how closely guarded the shooter is and the person shooting the ball must all be considered. The following are generally considered poor shot selections: forced shots when closely defended, shots that aren't regularly practiced but invented in the moment, shots taken too early in the possession before an offense develops, shots taken with no offensive rebounders available, shots taken out of comfortable range, shots taken too quickly late in a game with a tenuous lead and shots taken in critical situations by low percentage shooters. Determining what constitutes a good shot can sometimes be difficult. There are some gray areas that always exist. Good teams always have an awareness of good shot selection, but great teams never take bad shots. Great shot selection produces a significant competitive edge.

TWITTER WISDOM: "The main ingredient of stardom is the rest of the team." – John Wooden

DECEMBER 1

BIRTHDAY: Gary Payton Jr. 92, Rakeem Christmas 91

CLUTCH

Jerry West was known as "Mr. Clutch." His last second heroics for the Los Angeles Lakers became legendary and the NBA selected his image for their logo. Why do some players rise up and respond at crunch time while others shrink and fail. No matter how hard teams play throughout a game, during crunch time players become adrenalized. Speed and reaction-time increase, hands are quicker and jumping becomes more explosive. With time running out, the pressure to win affects breathing and heart rates. These physical changes in the body can imperceptibly affect the delicate calculations necessary for shooting and passing accuracy. Players who cultivate calmness in these situations seem to thrive. Players who are unafraid of failure often fail the least. Confidence and self-possession come from a simple decision to ignore imaginary consequences, to breathe calmly and to deliberately relax.

TWITTER WISDOM: "He who conquers others is strong; he who conquers himself is mighty." - Lao Tzu

YOUTUBE ASSIST – Robert Horry, A Great Clutch Shooter, "SwtSiamese21" 8:37

DECEMBER 2

BIRTHDAY: Brandon Knight 91, Ralph Beard 27

SHOT FEQUENCY PRACTICE

Shooting gurus address balance, grip, release, arc and follow-through. They incorporate dozens of creative drills to produce a volume of repetitive shots to develop muscle memory. One consideration that is often overlooked is practicing shots according to the average frequency with which they occur during a game. In a shooting drill, a player might find his groove early or late in the drill. Stringing a few 'made baskets' together produces an illusion of mastery. In a real game, shots occur as independent events with time gaps ranging from 45 seconds to several minutes to perhaps an hour or more considering the length of some TV games. Occasionally, a serious player should devise a personal workout that simulates the shot frequency that they take over the course of a game (or at least a half). By incorporating ball-handling, defensive slides, cardio and mixing in 'single shot events' from likely spots on the floor, players will approximate game conditions with much more accuracy.

TWITTER WISDOM: "Win, lose or draw the next day is a new day. Your next opponent could care less what happened between you and your last opponent." Derek Jones

DECEMBER 3

BIRTHDAY: Lindsey Hunter 70, Mike Bantom 51

SMART FOUL – DUMB FOUL

Committing a foul is not always a bad thing. When trailing in the last two minutes of a game, a coach may instruct players to foul in order to stop the clock hoping to trade 0, 1 or 2 points for 3's. Great comebacks often result from opposing teams choking at the foul line. Sometimes fouling a player on a break-away forces the player to make two shots from the foul line instead allowing a simple layup. The same can be said about putting a poor shooting big man to the foul line instead of allowing an easy put-back on a rebound. Coaches and players must always weigh the disadvantage of accumulating personal fouls on key players, however, committing smart fouls can definitely be a helpful strategy.

Dumb fouls occur all the time. Players will often try to 'make up' for an errant pass or missed shot by overcompensating with stupid aggressiveness. Jumping over a player's back to retrieve your missed shot, or lunging to steal the ball back after a bad pass is simply a foolish lack of discipline. Also, when your team has the lead down the stretch and the opponent is scrambling to get back into the game, do not foul a shooter or penetrator. This only helps the other team by stopping the clock which allows them to regroup, set up a press and substitute key players.

TWITTER WISDOM: "Be hard to play against but easy to play with." – Roger Goodling

DECEMBER 4

BIRTHDAY: Andre Roberson 91, Corliss Williamson 73, Jerome Lane 66 *Bernard King 56, Dick Ricketts 33

GETTING BENCHED

How you respond to being benched is a choice and reveals volumes about your character. Everyone has feelings. Everyone is sensitive to their status as a team member. Players who throw towels, pout or slouch on the end of the bench are children with stunted emotional growth. Mature players stay engaged and stay ready. They continue to contribute through encouragement and helpful comments to their teammates. If your playing-time is significantly decreased at some point in the season, the absolute best approach is to continue to hustle and be a positive practice player. Stay strong mentally, don't cave to the powerful impulses of jealousy and resentment. Fight through this dark time. Sometimes coaches reconsider their decisions and look at players differently later in the season. You make it much easier to be re-inserted if you've been a great teammate all along. Let the following question be a guiding principle: HOW DO YOU WANT TO BE REMEMBERED?

TWITTER WISDOM: "You have a choice to make when you're not playing. Either you're invested and a great teammate, or you're not." – Brad Stevens

DECEMBER 5

BIRTHDAY: Tina Charles 88, Josh Smith 85, Eddie Curry 82, Butch Lee 56, Muffet McGraw 55

GROOVING YOUR SHOT

Everybody can shoot, not everybody can MAKE. Part of preparing to play is going through the steps to groove your shot. Your shot can be affected by any part of your body from your toes to the tilt of your head. Re-creating the perfect form and release should be the goal. Take some time to properly warm-up and stretch, paying particular attention to shoulder, wrist and ankle joints. Awaken the nerve endings in your hands and fingers by alternately slamming the ball into each one. Rehearse a few slow motion shots into the air using only your shooting hand. Make intentional mental notes on your knee dip, the release point on your forefinger and the backspin of the ball. This process is akin to golfers taking numerous practice swings before putting, or baseball hitters checking all of their mechanics while they are in the on-deck circle. Always begin shooting close to the basket and work your way out to the three point line. Players who immediately hoist up shots from the three point line lose the chance to precisely calibrate their brains. Shooting is a delicate and fickle skill. Bring as much deliberate preparation to every shooting session as you can.

TWITTER WISDOM: "Confidence is built with continual, unrelenting effort. It does not precede accomplishment any more than a victory lap precedes the race." Ken Mannie

YOUTUBE ASSIST – Black Jack Shooting Video, "Jack Ryan" 8:28

DECEMBER 6

BIRTHDAY: Giannis Antetokounmpo 94

ACADEMIC GUTS

'Having Guts' is simply defined as "making yourself DO what you DON'T want to do." More formal synonyms include courage, fortitude and mettle. Taking a charge, diving for a loose ball and playing through exhaustion require courage and the character to accept the physical pain. These same principles are at play in the classroom. Forcing yourself to excel in school takes guts as well. Step one requires an attitude check. Instead of adopting the easy default position of the herd by complaining that school is boring, become open to curiosity and wonder. Understand that every subject you take is flammable. There are people whose intellects have been set on fire by these disciplilnes and have devoted their lives to discovering new insights. Just look for one tiny spark.

Step two requires some basic discipline. Come to class prepared. Always have a pen/pencil/notebook/laptop/i-pad or whatever technology allows for later retrieval of information. Choose a seat in the FRONT ROW. There are fewer distractions and you stay engaged. Be aware of your posture. Sit up straight and don't slouch. Step three requires that you FOLLOW-THROUGH on homework and assignments. Show some guts. Carve out time in your day to complete daily assignments. Step four is the most important. Do NOT allow peers to shame you for trying to be a good student. Their scorn is repressed admiration.

TWITTER WISDOM: "Hard subjects train the mind, hard exercise trains the body, hard people train the heart, hard times train the spirit. Do the hard things." @Edlatimore

DECEMBER 7

BIRTHDAY: Al Thornton 83, *Larry Bird, Max Zaslofsky 25

TIME MANAGEMENT

Write it down. Put a calendar in a prominent place in your room or use a white board, school planner or smart phone to keep track of assignments, homework, appointments, practices, and games. Every Sunday night map out a 'game plan' for the week. Anticipate your busiest times so that long range projects don't get backed up. Procrastination is one of life's greatest 'stress' producers. Attack your most difficult tasks first when the will and energy are at their highest levels. Chunk your more complex assignments into smaller manageable increments. Chip away at the mountain. Get a sense of accomplishment by just getting started.

TWITTER WISDOM: "Procrastination is one of the most common and deadliest of diseases and its toll on success and happiness is heavy." – Wayne Gretzky

DECEMBER 8

BIRTHDAY: Dwight Howard 85, Teresa Weatherspoon 65, Ken Durrett 48, Bob Love 42

LEADERSHIP

There is an old saying that states, "Lead, follow or get out of the way." Leaders come in all shapes, sizes and temperaments; but they all have one thing in common – THEY INSPIRE. Leadership is not some magical speech from a movie script. Leadership is in the "work." Leaders have an unshakeable vision and commitment to team goals. Their lives and actions scream out who they are louder than any words could do. We admire strong, decisive people who know where they are going and who can help others get there with them.

TWITTER WISDOM: "Team Leaders: your teammates need far less of hearing you lead than they do SEEING you lead." – Don Meyer

DECEMBER 9

BIRTHDAY: Kelly Oubre 95, Eric Bledsoe 89, Gerald Henderson 87, Otis Birdsong 55, World B. Free 53 *Cliff Hagan 31

THE IDEAL RECRUIT

If you are lucky enough to have the talent, skill and potential to play at a higher level, here are a few thoughts to enhance your attractiveness as a recruit. Project a personality of courtesy and thoughtfulness. Listen attentively and be grateful that any school is showing interest. Aside from uncommon competitiveness, display a disciplined demeanor on the court. Recruiters observe all behavior and will watch how you interact with teammates, referees, opposing players and fans. They observe how you walk to the huddle for timeouts, how closely you pay attention in the huddle, how you treat the managers and assistant coaches. They will monitor your social media. They will talk with coaches, teachers, counselors and principals. After your campus visit, they will ask current team members their opinion of your potential as a teammate. However, when it comes down to awarding a scholarship between two players with similar skills, coaches will choose the one with the proven ability to do college coursework. If you are on the bubble, the player who knows how to study and compete in the classroom will get the nod every time.

TWITTER WISDOM: "A coachable athlete is humble, disciplined and open to criticism and feedback. No matter how great they become, they remain committed to their own personal development." - Alistair McCaw

DECEMBER 10

BIRTHDAY: Dion Waiters 91, Mark Aguirre 59

THE GAMER

Some people are great practice players. They play loose and confident, and they stroke the ball with uncanny accuracy; however, their level of performance falls off when they are playing in front of paying customers. There are also a few players who seem remarkably average to the casual observer but will excel under the bright lights of competition. What is behind this mystery? A 'gamer' is someone who consistently performs in crucial situations, who hits important shots, makes key steals, comes down with huge rebounds or makes lead-protecting foul shots. Gamers seem to process pressure differently. Perhaps they have perfected their fundamentals more completely. Perhaps they have visualized these moments more vividly. Perhaps their sense of anticipation is heightened in these moments, and their brains perceive solutions more quickly. Whatever combination of traits contribute to this phenomenon, the gamer is special.

TWITTER WISDOM: "Champions have to have last-minute stamina, they have to have the skill and the will. But will must be stronger than skill." – Muhammed Ali

DECEMBER 11

BIRTHDAY: Malcolm Brogdon 92, Rebekkah Brunson 81, Shareef Abdur-Rahim 76

PICK-UP BALL

Long before the micromanaged world of AAU, youth leagues, personal trainers and youtube, the outdoor playground was the ultimate training facility for aspiring ballers. Every small town or big city precinct or ward had their signature outdoor court where skills were honed and reputations born. Playground legends seeped into folklore like Greek heroes. The beauty of pick-up ball was the blended texture of age and skill. Young players observed and were schooled by older, stronger and smarter talent. The team that won held the court until they were defeated. Games were played with cutthroat competiveness because losing meant you had to sit indefinitely. These unsupervised competitive gatherings of young players were remarkable lessons in self-government. Players called their own fouls, disputes over contested out-of-bounds deflections were settled by consensus, and running scores were often challenged and quickly arbitrated by the players with the best memories. Pick-up games are still a staple of the basketball culture, but they are played mostly indoors and are less spontaneous. Every young player should seek-out these unstructured opportunities in order to test their wings, experiment with impunity and learn the language of teamwork.

TWITTER WISDOM: "We have got to use every opportunity to improve individually so we can improve collectively." – Nick Saban

DECEMBER 12

QUALITY VS. QUANTITY REPETITIONS

Don't get caught in the trap of believing that extensive hours on the court necessarily translates into effective improvement. Some players can accomplish more skill-growth in fifteen minutes of a planned sequential workout than others can in two hours of a half-paced, unfocused shoot-around. When ball-handling and shooting drills are done at game speed, the transfer benefits are unmistakable. Practicing under game-fatigue conditions provides a competitive edge. You are synching the mental with the physical and providing a special familiarity with late game conditions. Remember, practice does NOT make perfect, only PERFECT practice makes perfect.

TWITTER WISDOM: "Shooting 100 game speed shots is more valuable than 500 lazy shots. Lazy shooting is a waste of time" - Jeff Hornacek

DECEMBER 13

BIRTHDAY: Larry Kenon 52, *Gus Johnson 38

GET STRONGER

Increasing your strength is a vital component in your development as a player. A strong base and core along with arm and hand strength advance your basketball effectiveness in dramatic ways. Concentrated strength work will make you more explosive in first step quickness and leaping ability especially on second jump efforts. Hand and forearm strength keeps the ball from being wrested away on rebounds and tie-ups. Added strength helps you to fight through picks and screens and keeps you from being knocked off the ball when you are bumped and jostled while dribbling. Strength-work also increases endurance and mental toughness. Take advantage of strength experts who will tailor programs that are basketball specific. If you don't have the luxury of a strength coach simply go "old school." Crank out push-ups and chin-ups, use dumb bells, squeeze rubber balls, roll and unroll a brick or cement block attached by a rope to a broom stick. Skill alone can only take you so far. Sculpt your body to be warrior-ready.

TWITTER WISDOM: "Put simply, in most cases the reason you're slow is because you are weak." - @STACKMedia

YOUTUBE ASSIST – Top 5 Basketball Strength Exercises that Basketball Players should Be Doing: "I love basketball TV" 8:23

DECEMBER 14

BIRTHDAY: Robert Covington 90, Nicolas Batum 88, Tamecka Dixon 75, Anthony Mason 66

TRASH TALKING

Trash talking has existed forever. The most basic explanation for it revolves around the insecurity a player feels about his ability to let his performance do the talking. Verbal jabs and sarcastic assaults intended to distract or demean a fellow competitor reflect a fundamental weakness of character. Under the guise of 'trying to get into your head', the trash talker spews his lame insults which are rarely clever or inventive and which merely serve as "real time bulletin board material." Trash talk usually motivates the opponent instead of discouraging him/ her. In the heated moments of competitive battle, it is sometimes tempting to lash out and respond to a taunting opponent. Occasionally, there are legitimate provocations, but to initiate trash talking or to make it a pattern of your game is not only dishonorable but cowardly. Most trash talkers are hiding behind the safety net of game and school officials who they know will come to their rescue if an opponent chooses physical retaliation. Confident athletes recognize the trap of juvenile trash talkers and will not allow their emotions to be manipulated by this strategy of distraction.

TWITTER WISDOM: "Don't let anyone walk through your mind with dirty feet." – Dabo Swinney

DECEMBER 15

BIRTHDAY: Jahlil Okafor 95, Sophia Young 83, *Charlie Scott 48

FOUL SHOT DUPLICATION

Photocopy your foul shot. Develop a ritual that is faithfully re-created every single time you step to the line. Along with placing your foot at a predetermined point on the line, using an exact dribble count and completing every other step in your personalized routine, it is essential that a deep breath or two is incorporated into the ritual. Deep breathing relaxes the muscles and mind. Some players find that taking a few "air-shots" before the ball is handed to them provides a rehearsal for perfect mechanics. Consistent foul shooters often visualize a successful free throw they have made a thousand times – perfect release, perfect trajectory, the ball nesting softly through the net. Just remember that there is no defense trying to prevent this FREE throw. Duplicate your ritual with sacred fidelity. In case of a miss, just make a tiny recalibration of the gun-sight. Something must have jostled loose on that charge you took.

TWITTER WISDOM: "The stars get the headlines, but glue-guys get you in the winner's circle. I don't think you can win without having that kind of player." – Dick Vitale

YOUTUBE ASSIST - How to Make More Free Throws: Basketball Shooting Tips, "ShotMechanics" 6:35

DECEMBER 16

BIRTHDAY: Nigel Hayes 94, Cliff Robinson 66, Jeff Ruland 58, Orlando Woolridge 51, Jan van Breda Kolff 51

HOW TO WATCH A GAME ON T.V.

You can watch a game as a fan or as a player. You will either be the 'play-by-play' guy or the 'color-commentator. The 'play-by-play' guy follows the ball and gives the superficial details of who is dribbling, passing, shooting or rebounding and then reacts to the obvious good or bad play. The 'color' guy goes deeper and explains why a play worked or why a coach made a certain decision. He anticipates a coach's strategy and provides a rationale for decisions that players make during the heat of battle. The color guy also notices things that occur away from the ball such as defensive rotations, battles on the block for post position, effective screening, poor block-outs or guys leaking out for easy baskets. Young players should occasionally focus on a single player whose position they play. Study them on both offense and defense. Notice everything about them: shooting form, defensive stance, ball handling confidence, aggressiveness, court vision, communication with teammates and how they respond to pressure. Watching games with 'intentionality' can accelerate your development as a complete player.

TWITTER WISDOM: "Every choice, every decision, everything that we do every day, we want to be a champion." – Nick Saban

DECEMBER 17

BIRTHDAY: Buddy Hield 93, Albert King 59, Brad Davis 55

TRANSITIONING FROM AAU TO SCHOOL BALL

AAU ball and school ball have different structures, dynamics and goals. There is a huge spectrum of AAU competition based on talent, travel and level of tournament; but there are still some fundamental differences between the missions of school-sponsored teams and AAU teams. AAU teams are generally composed of players from several different schools and are required to play multiple games in a single day. The opportunity to gain invaluable game-situation experience is undeniable, but basic fundamental work is often ignored. AAU teams usually have far fewer practices and are therefore limited in the details of preparation afforded to school teams that can prepare specifically for an upcoming single contest. With AAU comes a little more freedom to play loose and to experiment in different systems. School ball, however, often conforms to a more rigid philosophy of defense, shot selection and fundamentals. School teams represent communities, receive far more local publicity and can spawn legendary memories revived at reunions fifty years later. It is important for players to recognize the differences between the two missions and to commit with complete immersion to whichever team they are currently playing on.

TWITTER WISDOM: "It takes 20 years to build a reputation, and five minutes to ruin it." – Peyton Manning

DECEMBER 18

BIRTHDAY: Charles Oakley 63, Bobby Jones 51, Gene Shue 31

BE A SPONGE

There is a sensitive period between 8th and 11th grade when a player develops at supersonic speed. Coordination, strength, skill and court awareness seem to align and a player makes unprecedented strides. When a player falls in love with the game, something akin to addiction occurs. This is the time to become a sponge and soak up every ounce of knowledge possible regarding how to play the game. Scour youtube for instructional videos, watch clips of past college and pro hall-of-famers, attend as many high school and college games as possible in your area and soak up the sights, sounds and popcorn smells. Study the players in your area that already have reputations and borrow little pieces of their game. Learn where the most competitive pick-up games are played and challenge yourself against the best competition. Read basketball articles on-line or even occasionally pick up a book or biography of a great player. You might gain some invaluable insight into how to get the most out of the journey you are now on.

TWITTER WISDOM: "My best skill was that I was coachable. I was a sponge and aggressive to learn. – Michael Jordan

DECEMBER 19

BIRTHDAY: Mo Williams 82, *Kevin McHale 57, *Arvydas Sabonis 64

UNCONVENTIONAL SKILL DEVELOPMENT

To get better at basketball you've got to play basketball; however, incorporating a few unconventional drills into your routine might enhance 'hand-eye' coordination or improve dexterity and focus. Skipping rope has always been a staple for boxers, and could quickly improve footwork and leg strength for basketball players. Advance rope-skippers can do amazing combinations of double jumps, scissor jumps, and other rope manipulation tricks. Learning to juggle tennis balls can improve touch, timing and anticipation. Another helpful drill is having someone intentionally throw bad passes at you. Stand with your back to a wall or fence and allow passes to be thrown at your feet, above your head, too far to the left or right or with too much velocity. Also, catching different size balls can improve feel and touch. Have someone throw a rapid fire succession of various sized balls at you (basketball, tennis ball, ping-pong ball, dodge ball). You will be forced to look the balls into your hands thus reinforcing a basic fundamental of successful reception. To stretch the imagination further you might want to spend some time learning to shuffle a deck of cards or hitting a speed bag.

TWITTER WISDOM: "Today I will do what others won't, so tomorrow I can accomplish what others can't." – Jerry Rice

DECEMBER 20

BIRTHDAY: De'Aron Fox 97

CREATE SCORING OPPORTUNITIES

A big misconception about creating your own shot is that it has to be done off the dribble. Having a killer 'cross-over' or a sneaky, explosive 'change-of-pace' can certainly create some separation from your defender, but there are other ways to get wide-open shots. Larry Bird was the ultimate master of creating his own shot even though his athleticism was woefully average. He never 'broke ankles' or turned on the 'after-burners' to blast past defenders. Instead, he used precisely timed cuts, effective rubs off of screens, pick and pops, aggressive post-ups and a brilliant array of shot and pass fakes. Bird did have some first-step quickness that he employed when a defender closed-out too quickly or when a player left his feet to block his deadly outside shot. His offensive I.Q. was off the charts because he could read what his defender was trying to take away, then reacted with a perfectly executed counter. It's easy to admire players who can ditch their defenders with speed and flash, but an astute observer admires the crafty scorer who employs his sophisticated knowledge of movement and deception to create his own shots.

TWITTER WISDOM: "Don't let winning make you soft. Don't let losing make you quit. Don't let your teammates down in any situation." – Larry Bird

DECEMBER 21

BIRTHDAY: The Game of Basketball 1891

VERBAL COMMUNICATION

Great teams don't just communicate with each other they over-communicate with each other. A team committed to constant verbal sharing will make fewer mistakes in coverage and execution. Calling out blind screens or yelling "wolf" to alert a dribbler that a defender is sprinting up from behind are two of the most basic ways that players should use their voices. Some teams insist on the repetitive chirping of one syllable terms when practicing their man-to-man coverage – BALL (when covering the ball) DENY (when one pass away) HELP (when two or more passes away) DEAD (when a dribbler picks up his dribble). When defending a fast break, one player must always declare who's going to stop the ball handler. Players that switch on screens must loudly yell "switch" to eliminate any confusion. When one player is unaware of a defensive change, the entire team should be blamed. Every player should know who he/she is guarding at all times. Sometimes during multiple substitutions, mix-ups occur. While lined up for a foul shot, good teams are always pointing to the men they are guarding and communicating words of reinforcement about blocking out or watching out for a press. When a play is called from the bench, there should be a relay among every player on the floor to ensure everyone is ready for perfect execution. Teams that talk increase their competitive edge.

TWITTER WISDOM: "A great unit, whether it be football or any organization, shares the same heartbeat." – Bear Bryant

DECEMBER 22

BIRTHDAY: Dave Robisch 49, Tom Hawkins 36

SLOW MOTION REHEARSAL OF FUNDAMENTALS

Olympic gold medalist and world professional boxing champion Andre Ward mastered every technique of his sport. Until the day he retired, he would rehearse his punches in slow motion as part of his warm-up routine. Every jab, upper cut, hook and cross were slowly and meticulously executed with thoughtful deliberation concentrating on perfect form and balance. Training your muscle-memory with this kind of intentional focus pays dividends. Every basketball fundamental can be executed in this way as well, from pivoting, jump-stopping, defensive slides, live ball moves and shooting form. Slow it down to clean it up.

TWITTER WISDOM: "The more complete player I can be, the better those around me will be." – Brandon Ingram

DECEMBER 23

BIRTHDAY: Myke Henry92, Dave Lattin 43

COACHABILITY VS. TEACHABILITY

Both of these traits are vitally important to success in any team sport. Coachability is a willingness to receive both instruction and correction. Players who are open to change and who "buy in" to the culture, schemes and strategies always prosper inside a system. Players who resist even passively create unwanted tension. Stubbornness is often a form of selfishness. Coachable players use eye contact and respectful body language. It's possible, however, for a player to be coachable but not teachable. A coachable and physically talented player occasionally has trouble grasping all of the details and nuances of timing, movement and options of a complex system. Confusion can cause delayed reaction and a breakdown in team execution resulting in disastrous possessions. If your playing-time is being penalized because of this reason, there is an easy fix. Ask questions, pay attention, study game film and make it your mission to master every aspect of the system. Basketball is not brain surgery.

TWITTER WISDOM: "I do what I'm coached to do. That's part of being a team leader and captain. The job will change week in and week out, and it's not for you to question what your job is - it's to go out there and execute your assignments." – Larry Fitzgerald

DECEMBER 24

BIRTHDAY: Paul Pressey 58

CLOSE-OUT MECHANICS

One of the most important defensive fundamentals is the "close-out." Help-side responsibilities can pull a defender away from the man he/she is guarding. When the ball is quickly reversed or skipped back to his/her man, a defender is vulnerable. Learning to close-out 'under control' prevents penetration while at the same time discourage an outside shot. The following mechanics should be employed on all close-outs: 1. Sprint half-the distance to your man. 2. Simultaneously, raise your arms and palms away from your body and toward the opponent (this gives the illusion of being a little bit nearer to the opponent) while throwing your weight and shoulders behind your hips as you 'brake' in a sneaker-squeaking stutter step. 3. Arrive in a defensive stance with your weight on your heels, palms raised and ready to react to a drive or to challenge a shot. Recovering to guard your man without discipline often has disastrous results. The opponent either drives around you because you're off balance, or you get faked off your feet by the flimsiest of shot fakes.

TWITTER WISDOM: "Don't look for the big, quick improvement. Seek the small improvement one day at time. That's the only way it happens-and when it happens, it lasts." – John Wooden

DECEMBER 25

BIRTH: Eric Gordon 88, *Lefty Driesell 31*

HOW TO BECOME YOUR COACH'S FAVORITE PLAYER

1. Arrive early to practice and stay late. 2. Generate energy and enthusiasm in practice. 3. Pay attention in the huddle by listening with your eyes. 4. Cheer for your teammates when you are not in the game. 5. Be polite to those who can be of no use to you. 6. Do the dirty jobs of winning – defense, charges, sprinting back on defense. 7. Never make an excuse – accept correction with eye contact and a nod. 8. Don't be a clown or jerk in the locker room. 9. Don't be a distraction in the class room. Behave and perform so teachers make it a point to initiate a compliment about you to your coach. 10. Hit the winning shot against your rival.

TWITTER WISDOM: "Do your role as well as you possibly can and become a superstar in that role. Give it everything you got." – Brad Stevens

DECEMBER 26

BIRTHDAY: Tim Legler 66

PASSION

Two of the sweetest words a basketball coach can hear are "Gym Rat." To the coach it signals a player who is compelled to work constantly at the game he/she loves. Gym rats can spend lonely, isolated hours shooting and retrieving without the voice of another human being. Passion is the daily enthusiasm one brings to the mission of pursuing perfection. To be passionate about something is a gift you give yourself and everyone around you. All humans are affected and inspired when they are in the presence of passion. People admire and are drawn to the joy of enthusiasm in any pursuit. Constantly throw logs on your fire, bring your passion to an orange heat.

TWITTER WISDOM: "Each of us has a fire in our hearts for something. It's our goal in life to find it and keep it lit." – Mary Lou Retton

YOUTUBE ASSIST - NO EXCUSES - Best Motivational Video, "Ben Lionel Scott" 3:19 (some blunt language)

DECEMBER 27

BIRTHDAY: Kevin Ollie 72, Bill Self 62, Mark Few 62, Kent Benson 54, Rich Jones 46

HAND-OFF TECHNIQUES

For want of a nail, the shoe was lost;
For want of the shoe, the horse was lost;
For want of the horse, the rider was lost;
For want of the rider, the battle was lost;
For want of the battle, the kingdom was lost;
And all from the want of a nail.

Sometimes the most insignificant mental lapse can have a profound consequence in a game. Mastering the mundane details of handing off the ball to a teammate may seem insignificant, but if that fundamental is botched near the end of a close game the result can be costly. Once you receive the ball and a teammate approaches for a hand-off there are three critical steps: 1. Hold the ball close to your body. 2. Pivot to screen the on-coming defender with your hip in order to momentarily chip him/her away from your teammate. 3. Simultaneously, hold the ball on the platter of your hand and suspend it in the air at the moment the teammate is in position. Beautiful, seamless handoffs can lead to excellent offensive advantages. Sloppy, careless hand-offs can lead to disastrous turnovers.

TWITTER WISDOM: "If you don't have time to do it right, when will you have time to do it over? – John Wooden

DECEMBER 28

ATTACKING GAPS IN ZONES

Distort the zone. Stretch it, compact it, over-load it by ball and player movement. The most efficient distortion technique is for a player to attack the gaps with a dribble. This strategy will draw two and sometimes three defenders out of position attempting to slow down the penetration. There is certainly some risk because four to six arms and hands will be seeking to strip or deflect the ball, but the rewards far outweigh the risk. Selective but aggressive penetration of gaps in a zone creates a string of immediate defensive adjustments thus weakening the zone by forcing longer recovery distances. One or two extra passes often results in an uncontested shot.

TWITTER WISDOM: "I think sometimes in life the biggest challenges end up being the best things that happen in your life." – Tom Brady

YOUTUBE ASSIST - 3 Simple Keys to Score on a 2-3 Zone Defense: Basketball Moves For Beginners, "ShotMechanics" 7:28

DECEMBER 29

BIRTHDAY: Ron Perry 49

TRAITS OF A GREAT CAPTAIN

Team captains should be appointed not voted on. Team captains should be in complete alignment with the coach's philosophy and be an extension of the coach out on the floor. Team captains should be a model of confidence and positivity and be willing to make personal sacrifices for the good of the team. Team captains do not have to be vocal cheerleaders, but they must speak up at critical times. Team captains must be totally immersed in the culture of effort and competitiveness. Team captains set the tone for every practice by an unflagging commitment to excellence. Team captains must be the spokesman and the liaison to the coaching staff when an issue requires adult input. Team captains are sometimes not the official team captains. They may not be the ones who ceremoniously meet with the referees at midcourt before the game. Instead, they are the voices that teammates actually listen to.

TWITTER WISDOM: "Players that let teammates slide, coast or cut corners are just as responsible for failure as they are. STAND UP for SUCCESS!" –Tom Crean

DECEMBER 30

BIRTHDAY: Lebron James 84, Kenyon Martin 77, Steve Mix 47

GUARDING THE PICK AND ROLL

Several strategies can be successful to thwart the pick and roll. Many teams automatically switch although this sometimes produces unwanted match-ups later in the possession. Some teams hedge high on the screener forcing the dribbler to arc higher allowing the defender time to fight through the screen. The hedger must then sprint back to the roll man. This requires some pinching toward the key on the part of the other three defenders not involved in the pick and roll. A defender can also go under the screen and pick up the dribbler on the other side if the screening action is out of a shooter's range. A final strategy is the automatic double-team. Jumping the dribbler with both defenders disrupts the offense. The other defenders must immediately rotate into a three man zone protecting the basket or anticipating a steal. Of course all double teams are gambles because they create unbalanced numbers closer to the basket. A team must pick a strategy and be consistent in its execution.

TWITTER WISDOM: "Ultimately, that's what makes it fun, when you get them to the point where you're doing it together." – Steve Kerr

DECEMBER 31

BIRTHDAY: Brent Barry 71, Byron Russell 70, Tyrone Corbin 62

DEALING WITH A DIRTY PLAYER

Invariably, the person who retaliates is the one who gets caught. The best advice when confronted by an opponent who resorts to dirty play is to simply "play through it." Of course, if the dirty play is intolerable (sneaky elbows, extended knees on picks, stepping on feet, grabbing jerseys, undercuts on layups) then you and your coach must intervene by bringing it to the attention of the referees and/or the opposing coach. You must repress the urge to retaliate although it feels completely natural. Anger and pride make us do irrational things that can backfire. Getting ejected or suspended from future games is a high price to pay for stooping to the level of a cowardly opponent.

TWITTER WISDOM: "Discipline is not a light switch. Discipline is a way of life." – John Harbaugh

JANUARY 1

BIRTHDAY: Glen "Big Baby" Davis 86, Chris Webber 73, Mike Mitchell 56, Jimmy Jones 45

BLOCKING OUT
PERSONAL PROBLEMS

A common phrase used by a frustrated coach is "get your head in the game." Everybody's concentration can falter at some point. Some players are better than others at maintaining a high level of intensity night in and night out, but be aware of subtle subconscious issues that can interfere with optimal performance. When one's personal life is not in harmony, one's on-court performance can suffer, and the athlete is clueless to its cause. Some players who experience dysfunction in their lives decide to simply "lose" themselves in the game and make the competitive arena a refuge of total escape from the distractions of life. If home or school issues are present in your life, you don't have to let them color your performance. Acknowledge them, then put them on hold for an hour and a half so you can experience the joy of a head-first plunge into the fray.

TWITTER WISDOM: "It is what it is. But, it will be what you make it." – Pat Summitt

JANUARY 2

BIRTHDAY: Kirk Hinrich 81, Mike Newlin 49

AVOIDING SHOOTING INCONSISTENCY

It is truly weird how a player can be on fire on Tuesday night, and polar ice-cap cold two nights later. What changed? There might be a defender with more quickness and length, different distances for each open shot, different time-intervals between shots in the game, different defensive strategies, different game tempos and different shooting rhythms that make it impossible to duplicate the accuracy from the previous game. However, there are a few things that a player can control to increase shooting consistency. 1. Execute your warm-up routine with faithful detail making sure that all joints are properly limbered. 2. Pay attention to all parts of your mechanics. Visualize successful shots. 3. Make sure you are getting your legs into the shot. 4. Don't let early misses psyche you out. According to the law of statistics, a string of makes is right around the corner. 5. An aggressive drive and layup can take the lid off the rim, as can a couple of successful free throws. 6. Finally, spending a few minutes on the bench watching the game unfold can sometimes change a shooter's frame of mind and he/she might re-enter the game with a more accurate touch.

TWITTER WISDOM: "Until your will to prepare is greater than your will to win, you'll never tap your fullest potential." Coach Able @ TCTiger

JANUARY 3

BIRTHDAY: Rondae Hollis-Jefferson 95, Doug McDermott 92, Cheryl Miller 64

HOW TO COACH YOUR PARENTS

Unquestionably, the most important people in your life are the adults who are raising you. The amount of energy, attention and nurturing required to raise a pathetically helpless infant into a responsible adult is staggering. Occasionally, however, your guardians might be slightly misguided in the intensity of their involvement and can unintentionally bring some negative pressure by their comments, criticism and public behavior. Small doses of negative parent behavior is natural. Their interest begins and ends with your well-being, and team goals are often secondary to them. It is important to regularly convey to them the mission of the team, to clarify the role on the team that you have embraced, and to regularly display the joy you feel in being part of a unit. If you are subjected to regular critiques on the ride home, or if a parent's embarrassing behavior at games gets out of hand, you may need to confront the problem with calm but direct observations about how you are affected. Upon occasion the role of authority figure can be reversed and the child can teach the parent. In a perfect world, the insufferable parent becomes enlightened, and on the ride home even after a loss will limit his/her comments to a simple, "Have I told you how much I enjoy watching you play?"

TWITTER WISDOM: "I'm not sure why little league games have umpires behind the plate....The parents in the bleachers can see the strike zone way better apparently." Vernon Griffith

JANUARY 4

BIRTHDAY: Al Jefferson 85, Cliff Levingston 61

CLIQUES ON TEAMS

Cliques occur in every social situation. People gravitate into little pods of like-minded friends that they enjoy being with or who share their values. If a teammate thinks he/she acquires heightened social importance merely by associating with a certain group, that player is shallow and delusional. For the most part, cliques on teams are natural groupings that quickly evaporate once the jump-ball is tossed into the air. The problem with cliques is that sometimes players allow resentment and suspicion to fester because of real or imagined snubs or slights. It's hard for teenagers to realize that strong, secure people ignore the pettiness of imaginary social rankings.

TWITTER WISDOM: "You don't worry about fitting in when you're custom made." William Belliford

JANUARY 5

BIRTHDAY: Tyler Ulis 96, *Alex English 54, Rick Mount 47

BEING A DEFENSIVE PEST

What's more annoying than having an aggressive bee whiz around your head? You swat, duck and run. A defender who is constantly chopping his feet, making you change directions with your dribble, denying you the ball, stabbing at your dribble and smothering you when you pick up the ball can have the same distracting effect as a 'yellow-jacket.' Players like this are major disruptors. They interrupt your flow, hack your poise and make you want to fight. More importantly, the rest of the team feeds off their pesky energy as the turnovers multiply. If you have the skill and mentality to be a defensive pest, you need to cultivate it and bring that special value to your team.

TWITTER WISDOM: "Strength of will is essential to your survival and success. The competitor who won't go away, who won't stay down, has one of the most formidable competitive advantages of all." – Bill Walsh

YOUTUBE ASSIST - How to Stand Out on Defense | Game Time "PGC Basketball" 2:45

JANUARY 6

BIRTHDAY: Will Barton 91, Gilbert Arenas 82, Dwayne "Pearl" Washington 64

WHEN THE AIR GOES OUT OF THE BALL

No air, no bounce. No bounce, no play. It happens to every player at some point in their career. One's identity is no longer defined by the term "ball player." We move on and must devote our energies to a career and/or family. What transferable skills did playing sports give you? The cliché answers of course are discipline, teamwork, competitiveness and problem solving. A more hidden answer is "grit." Devoting yourself to the pursuit of excellence enhances a special resilience to setbacks. Fighting through obstacles and discouragements, pushing through fatigue and pain, battling through injury and disappointment was the perfect training ground for life. In addition, you will carry a bank of memories and friendships throughout the rest of your life. Hopefully, you cultivated other real life skills along the way: reading, communication (writing, speaking), critical thinking and positive social interaction.

TWITTER WISDOM: "Be the best version of yourself. Have passion, a great attitude, a single-minded focus, relentless energy, and always finish." – Jason Garrett

JANUARY 7

BIRTHDAY: JamesOn Curry 86, Coppie Pondexter 83, Todd Day 70

GUARDING A 2-ON-1 FASTBREAK

If you are the back man on the press and confront a 2 on 1 fast-break you must be smart. You are the GOALIE who must protect the basket. Retreat deep into the lane and fake-jab at the approaching dribbler trying to bait an extra pass. Your whole job is to prevent a lay-up. NO LAY-UP. Too often the lone defender is sucked out too far toward the ball-handler thus creating a passing angle past his ear for a lay-up. Fake-jabbing and a quick retreat can force an extra pass, slow down the break, and create a shot-pass decision. A 7-foot pull-up jumper is a much lower percentage shot than a lay-up. This strategy might also give your teammates an extra second to 'get back' and help out.

TWITTER WISDOM: "People have no idea how many times you have to finish second in order to finish first." – Jack Nicklaus

YOUTUBE ASSIST – Learn Geno Auriemma's 2-on-1 Rules! Basketball 2017 #7, "ChampionshipProductions" 5:08

JANUARY 8

BIRTHDAY: Willie Anderson 67, Calvin Natt 57

USE THE BOARD

The coaching mantra 'use the board' has echoed inside every gym since a peach basket was mounted on a wall at the Springfield, Massachusetts YMCA. The reason is basic. The ball seems to go into the basket at a higher percentage than when it is simply flipped over the lip of the rim. Putting the ball higher on the board takes it out of the range of most shot blockers, and missed attempts tend to allow a little more time for a crashing offensive rebounder to gauge the carom off the rim. Admittedly, as basketball evolves, this mantra does not ring as absolute as it once did. Dunks, floaters and baby hooks are now potent offensive weapons that do not depend on the backboard, but this wisdom still holds true for full-speed layups by young non-dunkers, power moves by inside players and most 'put-backs' around the rim.

TWITTER WISDOM: "Run from being good. Chase being great." – Chip Kelly

JANUARY 9

BIRTHDAY: Michael Beasley 89, Muggsy Bogues 65, M.L. Carr 51

PLAY TO YOUR STRENGTHS

Everyone cannot be an 'all-around' basketball player who can shoot, defend, rebound, dribble and pass with deadly effectiveness. Each of us have strengths that contribute to victory, and weaknesses that can be exploited. Know who you are and take extreme pride in the unique qualities you bring to the team. There are some very important intangibles that are not measured by the most sophisticated stats and analytics. No team keeps track of sprint times when getting back on defense, or proper screening angles, or block out-totals, or clean entry passes to the wing, or post feeds to the proper shoulder. Even a player with limited offensive skills can bring significant value by becoming a defensive specialist, an attacking rebounder or by setting monster picks. Basketball teams are not democracies. Every player is not guaranteed an equal number of shots. Try to perfect the things that you do best. Recognize, then relish your role.

TWITTER WISDOM: "It's not how big you are, it's how good you are." – Muggsy Bogues

JANUARY 10

BIRTHDAY: Glen Robinson 73, George Carter 44

PEER PRESSURE

Surprisingly, peer pressure will be present throughout your entire life; however, when you are young, you are the most susceptible to it. To be liked, to fit in, to be accepted by your peers, to avoid being laughed at, to rebel against old fashioned restrictions are all powerful impulses for every young person. The problem with caving into peer pressure is two-fold: 1. It often involves breaking the law (drugs, alcohol, vandalism). 2. It can be a regrettable betrayal of your core values. Develop the discipline of examining every choice you make. Listen for that feint buzzer in your conscience. Your friends do not have your goals and dreams in mind when they chip away at your resistance. The road to ruin is paved with the stones of careless judgement.

TWITTER WISDOM: "Do the right thing! If you have to think about it you shouldn't do it." – Pat Summitt

JANUARY 11

BIRTHDAY: Epiphanny Prince 88, Briann January 87, Tony Allen 82, Darryl "Chocolate Thunder" Dawkins 57

THE POWER OF VISUALIZATION

Your brain responds to an imagined success in an almost identical way that it responds to an actual success. Rehearsing successful attempts in your head with your eyes closed, produces surprising improvements. Scientific experiments with control groups have supported this theory. Random groups of people were selected to shoot foul shots, putt golf balls, throw darts etc. One group repeated the skill without visualization while the other group repeated the skill after a session of intense visualization of successful attempts. The second group's results were markedly improved. It appears that the brain records imaginary repetitions of success and transfers the information to the neurological system for future recall in real time. This is why some coaches will practice cutting down the nets, or having each player lift a trophy above their head before the team enters the playoffs. Visualization can help it come true.

TWITTER WISDOM: "Success occurs when your dreams get bigger than your excuses." – Zig Ziglar

JANUARY 12

BIRTHDAY: *Dominique Wilkins 60, Campy Russell 52

GIRL FRIEND - BOY FRIEND DRAMA

Just be careful. Young love can hit hard and athletic performance can soar or suffer. From Shakespeare to Freud no one has ever fully understood the mystery of love. During your playing days, emotions will affect your game. It's unavoidable. Stuff happens in life that we can't control. Everyone who has ever lived has been plagued by jealousy, suspicion, pride, slights, hurt feelings and arguments. It's the human condition and your unique personal pain and confusion is universal. Everyone eventually becomes a full-fledged, card-carrying member of the heart-break club. The only strategy that seems to stabilize the situation is to "name the feeling." Give an inner voice to how you are feeling so that it can be labeled and momentarily placed on a shelf in the fruit cellar of your mind. By pinpointing the source of your anxiety you can create a break in the clouds so that your athletic performance can lift-off for an hour or two.

TWITTER WISDOM: "You can't have a relationship without any fights, but you can have a relationship worth fighting for." Unknown

JANUARY 13

BIRTHDAY: Odyssey Sims 92, James Posey 77, *Tom Gola 33

FREE THROWS – REPETITION AND BREATH CONTROL

Making free throws contributes so significantly to victory that hours upon hours should be spent in perfecting technique and in cultivating confidence. An old synonym for the foul line is "the charity stripe," a term that acknowledges the gift of a free attempt with absolutely no defenders trying to impede your success. How can you explain why a great foul shooter misses a critical free throw? What conditions have changed? Did someone magically reduce the circumference of the hoop or tilt the rim upward. Was the shooter forced to move back a foot or two from the 15 foot distance? Does the gym's humidity or temperature drastically change in the moments before his/her release? No, the change occurs between the ears of the shooter. The heightened pressure of the shot causes some imperceptible changes in breathing and heart rate resulting in the misfiring of neurological synapses in the brain. Since these precise pressure situations cannot be duplicated in the gym laboratory, the tiniest miscalculation of distance, force or trajectory can result in mission failure. Breath control is the most potent antidote to pressure because it enhances relaxation. Always be aware of the value of slow, deep breathing.

TWITTER WISDOM: "It's about getting better at getting better." @ sportsmotto

YOUTUBE ASSIST - Ugliest Free Throw Shooting Form in NBA History, "Hoops Fun" 6:44

JANUARY 14

BIRTHDAY: Aaron Brooks 85, Swen Nater 50, Wayne Hightower 40, Kenny Sailors 21

PLAYING MULTIPLE SPORTS

The benefits of playing multiple sports as you grow up far outweigh the advantages gained by obsessive specialization. Every sport places widely different emphasis on muscle groups, hand-eye coordination, endurance demands, reaction situations and exposure to various coaching styles. Playing multiple sports improves your entire package of athletic capabilities. Psychologically, shifting seasons can provide the break needed to return energized and eager. Be leery of coaches and adults who suggest that specialization is in your best interest. If you have a passion for basketball, you can still hone your skills each day with abbreviated workouts, but do not sacrifice the small window of life that gives you the opportunity to experience the thrill and joy of competition, friendships, experiences and memories.

TWITTER WISDOM: "The greatest compliment to any player is he is a great teammate. We can't all be great players, but we can all be great teammates." – Jay Bilas

JANUARY 15

BIRTHDAY: Ricky Sobers 53, Ernie Digregorio 51, *Bob Davies 20

DEVELOPING TEAM RITUALS

Humans are tribal. We evolved in small groups of related families that had to unite for safety and survival. Our impulse to identify with our tribe runs deep, and adopted rituals help to solidify that kinship. Teams dress in tribal uniforms and colors. Teams put their hands together and shout mission statements in ritual exits from huddles. Teams develop rituals around player introduction. These game-night rituals help to create bonds of loyalty and trust, but healthy rituals can also extend into how a team begins and ends practice, pre-game meals and many other tribal-bonding traditions. Embrace your rituals. They are your team's unique signature.

TWITTER WISDOM: "When you come to practice, you cease to exist as an individual. You're part of a team." – John Wooden

JANUARY 16

BIRTHDAY: Gerald Henderson 56

PUNCTUALITY

Be on time every time. Being habitually late is selfish and disrespectful. Making people adjust their lives to your schedule breeds resentment and erodes their opinion of your character. It may seem like a small thing, but this one trait is the first indicator of your trustworthiness. Being punctual is a hallmark of consideration for other people's time. Develop this discipline early in life. It will pay huge dividends later.

TWITTER WISDOM: "Players who are late are saying that their time is more important than the team." – Don Meyer

JANUARY 17

BIRTHDAY: Tyler Zeller 90, Dwyane Wade 82

PLAYING FOR A BAD COACH

The word 'bad' is vague and subjective. If your coach lacks knowledge, commitment and empathy you might be justified in using the label. If your coach is organized, implements a system and provides both correction and instruction to help the team improve, you need to reevaluate the talent level of you and your teammates. Some excellent coaches have mediocre coaching records, and some coaches who have won championships were simply in the right place at the right time. Their teams won despite the lack of coaching.

If you are stuck in a 'bad coach' situation don't waste your energy complaining and blaming circumstances out of your control. Practice hard, play hard and be a model teammate. Supply the positivity that might be missing. Sometimes a good captain can actually be the coach on the floor by holding his teammates accountable while inspiring them to play hard from the jump ball to the final horn. Sometimes living through a nightmare season is retrospectively an incredible learning experience.

TWITTER WISDOM: "One thing you can control is how hard you play, how much you give to the team, and how much you sacrifice for the team." – LeBron James

JANUARY 18

BIRTHDAY: Larry Smith 58, *Dino Meneghin 50

MENTORS AND ROLE MODELS

One of the most flattering and valuable experiences for a younger player is to be 'taken under the wing' of an older player who teaches you how to play the game. "Learning the ropes"` from an experienced mentor accelerates your development at warp speed. Observing and studying a talented player even from a distance provides a standard of aspiration. Don't be ashamed of being a wide-eyed fan of an older player in your program. When the opportunity arises ask him/her to demonstrate some specific move that you want to incorporate into your game. You will be surprised at how willing most players are to share their knowledge. Every great player in the world can point to someone whose style they imitated when they were young and incorporated much of that player's game into their own.

TWITTER WISDOM: "HS Athletes: When you're 25 you're going to realize that the people who demanded your best were also the ones who cared about you the most." - Matt Lisle

JANUARY 19

BIRTHDAY: Javale McGee 88, Michael Adams 63

CLASS

The word 'class' is hard to define. The word is perhaps a bit overused in sports journalism and broadcasting. Players are described as 'class-acts.' A gesture to help an opponent up from the floor is described as a 'classy-move.' Recognizing the efforts of your teammates in a post-game interview is a 'class' thing to do. The origins of this term; however, are somewhat sketchy. It's a reference to the behavior expected of a class of educated, well-bred and cultured elitists who have prescribed behaviors that supposedly separate them from the vulgar manners of the unwashed masses. Nevertheless, the word is used today in a glowingly positive context to describe a person who behaves with humility, unselfishness and regard for a fellow competitor. To be remembered as an athlete who conducted himself with class both on and off the court is the ultimate compliment. In the sometimes 'cut-throat' world of competitive sports, it may be difficult to maintain classy behavior night in and night out against ruthless opponents, but always strive for this gold standard of discipline. You will never regret it.

TWITTER WISDOM: "Risk more than others think is safe. Care more than others think is wise. Dream more than others think is practical. Expect more than others think is possible" - @sportsmotto

JANUARY 20

BIRTHDAY: Jason Richardson 81, Nick Anderson 68, Ron Harper 64, *Baily Howell 37

BUS RIDES

Bus rides can be long and dreadfully monotonous. Most players put on head-phones, nap or play games on their phones. Some laid-back quiet time is relaxing and mind-clearing. The forced isolation in your seat also affords some time to complete some homework or read a few pages of an assignment. Knocking off a small chunk of schoolwork is productive and satisfying. A bus trip is also a great time to visualize and mentally rehearse. It allows time to prepare intellectually for the game by re-reading a scouting report, familiarizing yourself with the individual tendencies of key opponents and discussing with team-mates a few details of the game plan. The team is trapped together on the bus. Why not use this time to further enhance the chances of victory. This tiny bit of extra preparation on the way to the game might be the difference between a miserable or joyful bus-ride home.

TWITTER WISDOM: "Freshmen want to play. Sophomores want to start. Juniors want to score. Seniors want to WIN!" – John Beilein

JANUARY 21

BIRTHDAY: Hakeem Olajuwon 63, Detlef Schrempf 63, Clifford Ray 49, John Chaney 32,

FOURTH-QUARTER LEGS

If you play the game hard, your body will be functioning differently in the fourth quarter. The depletion of nutrients and energy result in fatigued muscles responding with imperceptible changes. Experienced players understand their bodies and realize that tired legs can affect the precision of their shooting mechanics both from the floor and on the foul line. Tired players will not get quite as much lift on their jump shot and their arc may flatten in its trajectory. Tired players are also prone to commit more fouls. Like the championship rounds in boxing, the fourth quarter will be a test of wills and desire, and if two teams are equal in talent, the better conditioned team will have stronger legs and probably prevail.

TWITTER WISDOM: "It only takes a loss of about 2% of your body weight through sweat to start seeing a decrease in your athletic performance. Hydrate often!" - @VoltAthletics

JANUARY 22

BIRTHDAY: Dillon Brooks 96, Greg Oden 88, Carolyn Peck 66, Quintin Daily 61

COMFORT ZONE

GET OUT OF YOUR COMFORT ZONE. This is universal advice offered by every self-help book ever written. The only way a player can grow in skill and confidence is to keep expanding the boundaries of challenge. To get stronger one must increase the weight and reps in your workout. To develop endurance, one must increase the duration and intensity of your cardio work. To develop better ball-handling skills you must push yourself hard enough in your daily regimen so that the intensity and complexity of the drills produce mistakes while you are simultaneously increasing speed and finger strength. Seek out the best competition available. Find the most competitive pick-up games, challenge yourself against older, stronger players, get up before dawn for morning runs. It is easy to remain in the safety of the familiar. Expand, grow, risk failure. Those who work the hardest are the last to surrender!

TWITTER WISDOM: "I hate the feeling of going to bed at night when I don't feel like I pushed myself." – Steve Nash

JANUARY 23

BIRTHDAY: Larry Hughes 79, Sergei Belov 44

THE PRONOUNS I, ME, MY

Try to reduce the use of these three pronouns in your everyday conversation. Every topic does not have to circle back to your experiences and accomplishments. When you make a conscious attempt to refrain from trying to 'top' someone else's story, you become a better listener, a better teammate and less annoying.

TWITTER WISDOM: "Your team doesn't care if you are a superstar. They care if you are a super teammate." – Jon Gordon

JANUARY 24

BIRTHDAY: Mark Eaton 57,

PASSING ANGLES

If you have played pool or billiards, you understand the geometry of angles. Understanding passing angles in basketball is also critical. Passing from the correct angle results in successful completions that may lead directly to a score versus a deflection, interception or an impotent reception. Sometimes a mere lateral dribble away from the baseline provides a better angle to feed the post. Sometimes veering to the right or left while leading a fast break will create a better window to hit a teammate cutting to the hoop from an outside lane. Sometimes a quick reversal of the ball or a skip pass dramatically opens up better passing angles. Sometimes running the baseline when inbounding the ball after a score will create an easier angle to hit a teammate being face-guarded in a full-court press. It's a shame that Euclid lived before the game of basketball was invented, he'd have been a perennial all-star.

TWITTER WISDOM: "Be stubborn about your personal belief in yourself." Merlin Olson

YOUTUBE ASSIST - How to Pass a Basketball: Top 5 Passing Tricks, Tips, and Highlights, "ShotMechanics" 7:21

JANUARY 25

BIRTHDAY: Chris Mills 70, Byron Beck 45, *Dick McGuire 26

BODY LANGUAGE

Everyone is bi-lingual. You speak a native language out of your mouth, but you convey a ton of other revealing information from your "body language" which is universally understood. Body language sends both conscious and subconscious messages to your coaches, fans and teammates. Avoid negative body language – slouching posture on the bench, putting your head down after a mistake, showing facial displeasure when a teammate commits an error, looking away from your coach when he/she is speaking to you, flippantly throwing the ball to a referee, slamming the ball down on the floor when called for a foul, clapping in the face of an opponent, lying on the floor too long after a minor injury in order to get sympathy from the crowd.

Cultivate positive body language – run over to help a teammate get up from the floor, hand-clap to inspire more hustle from your team-mates, stride confidently to the foul line, hustle over to the huddle during a timeout, be completely engaged while sitting on the bench, keep your head up after making a mistake or when your team is get-ting blown out, make eye contact when you are being addressed by a coach, referee or peer; shake off a minor injury in order to continue to help your team, and finally, after a loss, walk out of the gym with a proud and erect posture because you gave your all.

TWITTER WISDOM: "Body language never whispers. It SCREAMS!"
– Buzz Williams

JANUARY 26

BIRTHDAY: Montrezl Harrell 94, Gerald Green 86, Vince Carter 77

DON'T TELEGRAPH YOUR PASSES

You'd think we'd have a more modern technological reference today for players who unwittingly reveal the direction of their passes. Don't 'instagram' your passes. Don't 'tweet' your passes. Don't 'message alert' your passes. Young players must realize that all 'telegraphing' is done with the eyes. Staring at your target while you wind up to heave a pass alerts not only your defender, but the defender of your intended receiver and the entire viewing audience in the stands. Learn to play with some sly peripheral vision. Scan the movement patterns in front of you and learn to detect openings and angles without direct eye-contact. Efficient football quarterbacks will purposely mislead defenders by looking at different sections of the field while intending to throw the ball to another specific spot. This same skill of 'looking-off' defenders works in basketball as well.

TWITTER WISDOM: "A star can win any game; a team can win every game." – Jack Ramsay

YOUTUBE ASSIST - Better Passing by Breaking Windows | Game Time | PGC Basketball, "PGC Basketball" 2:40

JANUARY 27

BIRTHDAY: Kristi Toliver 87, Tammy Sutton-Brown 78

JUMP STOP FOR
BALANCE AND SAFETY

The jump stop is the most basic fundamental of basketball. Playing off two feet is a simple yet crucial habit. Jump stop to receive a pass. Jump stop to avoid traveling. Jump stop to gather yourself for accurate layups, jump stop to retrieve a contested loose ball, jump stop to set a screen and jump stop to avoid committing a charge. The jump stop ensures a solid base that will eliminate or at least minimize many costly errors.

TWITTER WISDOM: "Every player goes to team practice - IT'S REQUIRED! It's what you do outside of what's required that separates you from the rest." Daniel Makepeace

JANUARY 28

BIRTHDAY: Andre Iguadala 84, Tony Delk 74, Michael Cage 62, Gregg Popovich 49

READ

Learning to read is the second greatest feat for any human being. Learning to speak is the first. Few people realize the enormous intellectual complexity involved in translating the symbolic squiggle-marks on a page into coherent meaning. Our meteoric rise as a species is directly related to compiling, then building on knowledge written down by previous generations. If deer had this capacity, they would teach their young about the danger of on-coming headlights, and they wouldn't look so stupid as we zoom toward them. Because reading requires a degree of mental energy, young people find it hard and often try to avoid it. Reading broadens your world. Reading makes YOU more interesting. Reading can improve your basketball game. There are dozens of magazines, on-line articles and blogs that specifically address basketball topics and profile rising stars in the game. There are some fascinating biographies of basketball legends like Pete Maravich, Wilt Chamberlain, Michael Jordan, Lebron James and Steph Curry that can inspire young players today. There are novels that contain riveting basketball themes. Read more. Explore more. Learn more. Grow more.

TWITTER WISDOM: "Success is found in your daily agenda. It's what you do on a daily basis that determines where you are heading in life." Allistair McCaw

JANUARY 29

BIRTHDAY: Marc Gasol 85, Greg Ballard 55

UNDERSTANDING TEMPO

Great teams have an awareness of clock and score especially down the stretch. Great teams can play both fast and slow depending on the situation. Great teams have strategies to speed up deliberate teams or slow down up-tempo teams. Players must have a feel for the flow of a game. Quick shots early in a possession with a tenuous fourth quarter lead can have disastrous consequences. Taking a few extra seconds to walk the ball up the court can milk the clock. Running an offense through its cycle a few times before taking a shot can put some tick-tocks in your pocket.

When playing from behind, the tempo must be increased. Full and half court presses, run and jumps, random double teams and selective fouling of bad foul shooters can produce a more chaotic pace. Experienced players will sense and respond to the changing tempos required to win games.

TWITTER WISDOM: "Magic exercises and gimmicky programs won't get you as far as fundamentals, studying, sleep, and eating right consistently." John Cissik

JANUARY 30

BIRTHDAY: Jalen Rose 73, Mychal Thompson 55, Tom Izzo 55

THE POISON OF JEALOUSY

Jealousy is a nasty toxin that can easily seep into any relationship. All humans experience this corrosive emotion at certain points in their lives. When jealousy creeps into the locker room because someone else is getting more playing time or scoring more points, team cohesion and performance will suffer. The mental energy wasted on being jealous is draining and becomes a festering distraction. Jealousy is a completely unproductive emotion because it only makes you miserable. Jealousy is powerless. Your jealousy cannot change the circumstances. It is amazing how much more can be accomplished when no one cares who gets the credit.

TWITTER WISDOM: "Those who waste their time comparing themselves to others have already lost the long game." @SquatUniversity

JANUARY 31

BIRTHDAY: Len Chappell 41, Johnny Egan 39

REBOUND WITH TENACITY

Come down with the dang ball! Grab it, snag it, snatch it, claim it – JUST GET IT. Too many balls are popped loose from the first person to get his hands on the rebound because of a little bit of contact. Two-handed rebounders are generally stronger and more consistent than one-handed, stretch-out rebounders. As you coil and spring for a rebound, anticipate a collision. Clamp the ball with pit bull tenacity. A little extra hunger to win the rebound can save a critical possession for your offense, or end a possession for your opponent. Once the ball is secure, make sure it is tucked tightly under your chin as you land. Chinning the ball makes it difficult for little guard-pests to strip it out of your hands.

TWITTER WISDOM: "So much of success is the second effort and multiple efforts. Just as these characteristics win games; they also translate to success." – Kevin Eastman

YOUTUBE ASSIST – Own the Offensive Glass with this drill from Shaka Smart, "Championship Productions" 4:35

FEBRUARY 1

BIRTHDAY: Kevin Martin 83, Robert "Tractor" Traylor 77

FEEDING THE POST

Fake high, pass low. Fake low, pass high. Move the defender's hands to create a passing window. Bounce passes are discouraged unless thrown along the baseline. When feeding from the corner take a dribble toward the wing then step through with the high leg to shield the ball. Hook a bounce pass with your thumb ending up pointed to the floor to create some 'English' allowing the ball to spin back toward the post man.

When no safe angle is available from the wing, quickly swing the ball to the top of the key. Post players should re-seal at a different angle, and the ball should be delivered with an air pass from above the head.

If the chemistry exists, a lob toward the back corner of the backboard will be successful if a fronted post player holds his seal then releases when the ball is directly over his head. Guards need to keep their big men happy by cultivating the art-form of post feeding.

TWITTER WISDOM: "If you drink enough water in the morning, you will feel happier, sharper, and more energetic throughout the day." - @Funnytruth

YOUTUBE ASSIST - Basketball Passing : Feed the Post in Basketball, "expertvillage" 2:36

FEBRUARY 2

BIRTHDAY: Sean Elliot 68

TAKING NOTES

When information travels through your ears, into your brain, down your arm and onto paper, the knowledge sticks more firmly in your mind. You also have created a resource that you can return to later to refresh your understanding of important information. Cultivate a habit of taking good notes whether with pen and paper, a laptop or phone. Some serious players keep a notebook by their bed to record thoughts and observations about the game they are trying to master. When you reach this level of intellectual dedication you are entering rarefied air as a player.

TWITTER WISDOM: "Champions play as they practice. Create a consistency of excellence in all your habits." – Mike Krzyzewski

FEBRUARY 3

BIRTHDAY: Robert Pack 69, Vlade Divac 68

TURNOVERS

Every turnover is a lost offensive possession. Turnovers are gifts that your opponent stole from your porch at Christmas time. Do not squander offensive possessions through careless mechanics and execution. Reducing shot attempts per possession can have disastrous results because even if the shot is missed, at least three positive things can happen: 1. The shooter could be fouled. 2. A teammate could get an offensive rebound. 3. A foul could be called on an opponent going for the rebound. Next to scoring, limiting turnovers is perhaps the most critical goal of every team, every game.

TWITTER WISDOM: "GREAT players use mistakes as motivation. AVERAGE players use mistakes as excuses." - Daniel Makepeace

FEBRUARY 4

BIRTHDAY: Malik Monk 98, Vern Fleming 62, *Neil Johnston 44

BOMBS AWAY – 3 POINT WISDOM

The three point shot revolutionized the game. Adding an extra point for a longer shot produced radical changes in strategy, created the opportunity for more dramatic comebacks and inflated individual stats. Most three pointers occur after penetration. Penetration forces help-side defense. If the man guarding you on the perimeter sinks to help, you need to read his head. Always drift away from his vision. He will waste precious time trying to find you once the ball is kicked out. One of the easiest ways to create a 3 pt. opportunity is after an offensive rebound. Very often perimeter defenders will either leak out toward their offensive end or drift toward the paint for long rebounds. In both cases the defender momentarily loses contact with the guy they are guarding. When this happens, the perimeter players need to quickly relocate away from the defender's vision. An alert offensive rebounder will pivot to find a three point marksman on the wing. This exact strategy can also be used whenever the ball enters the post at any point in the offensive flow. Fanning the ball to a three point shooter whose defender is sinking to help on the post creates great shots taken in rhythm. Finally, making that extra pass on defensive rotations can result in a shot that is wider open and has a higher percentage of splashing in for three. When a team is accurately dropping cluster bombs of three pointers, they are very hard to beat.

TWITTER WISDOM: "You're always doing one of two things as a player. You're either IMPACTING winning or COMPLICATING winning." – Tom Crean

FEBRUARY 5

BIRTHDAY: Terrence Ross 91, John Beasley 44

PLAYING ON A BAD TEAM

In the great book *MY LOSING SEASON,* legendary author Pat Conroy reveals the emotional travails of playing on a bad team. Sports are black and white. The scoreboard declares a winner and a loser, but do not fall into the easy trap of allowing an artificial label to define your identity. It's not always easy, but athletes must separate the team record from their own sense of worth. Even the greatest poker players are powerless when they are dealt a poor hand. It's always fun when your team wins, but true character is revealed when your team gets pounded night in and night out. Keep plugging, keep improving, keep competing. Humility is a beautiful quality that allows us to enjoy future successes more profoundly. Sometimes vain, arrogant and insecure athletes will avoid joining a team because they think the team won't be successful. They are afraid that their imaginary and flimsy reputations will be tarnished. Don't be a coward-puppet controlled by the strings of peer opinion. Always compete like a champion.

TWITTER WISDOM: "It is your response to winning and losing that makes you a winner or a loser." – Harry Sheehy

FEBRUARY 6

BIRTHDAY: Kevon Looney 96, Jonny Flynn 89, Kris Humphries 85, Eric Money 55

TEAM GUY OR ME GUY

A very successful coach once wrote that he paid attention to only three stats – charges, floor burns and stitches. He claimed that every other stat would take care of itself if his team focused on this kind of hustle and sacrifice. When a player seems unaffected by a team-defeat as long as he/she scored enough points, there is a problem. Don't deceive yourself into thinking that this self-absorbed attitude goes undetected by teammates. Selfishness is extremely hard to disguise; however, it would be disingenuous to suggest that a player should have no ego at all and be completely ignorant of his own "stat line." Just remember that basketball games are won because of multiple individual 'stat lines.' Michael Jordan did NOT win six NBA championships – the TEAMS he played on won six NBA championships.

TWITTER WISDOM: "Everyone on your team is important. Importance knows no rank." – Mike Krzyzewski

FEBRUARY 7

BIRTHDAY: Isaiah Thomas 89, Steve Nash 74, Juwan Howard 73

SEEK OUT THE NINJAS

Ancient ninjas were said to have supernatural powers along with some deadly efficient skills. Some of basketball's greatest players could be classified as modern ninjas. Study some of the ancient masters on youtube. Seek out highlights of the following:

POINT GUARDS: Nate 'Tiny' Archibald, Steve Nash, John Stockton, Allen Iverson, Isaiah Thomas (Detroit Pistons) and Kevin Johnson.

SHOOTING GUARDS: John Havlicek, Hal Greer, Dick Barnett, Bill Bradley, Joe Dumars, Mark Price, Byron Scott, Chris Mullin, Reggie Miller

POWER FORWARDS: Dan Issel, Dave Debusschure, Wes Unseld, Karl Malone, Dave Cowens, Darryl Dawkins, Kevin McHale, Maurice Lucas, Tim Duncan, Charles Barkley

CENTERS: Bill Russell, Nate Thurmond, Wilt Chamberlain, Kareem Abdul Jabbar, Elvin Hayes, Artis Gilmore, Bill Walton, Robert Parish, Hakeem Olajuwan, Shaquille O'Neal

SPECIAL NINJA BLACK BELTS – Connie Hawkins, George Gervin, Earl Monroe, Pete Maravich, Penny Hardaway, Julius Irving, Michael Jordan, Kobe Bryant and Magic Johnson

TWITTER WISDOM: "When you're good at something, you'll tell everyone. When you're great at something, they'll tell you." – Walter Payton

FEBRUARY 8

BIRTHDAY: Klay Thompson 90, Alonzo Mourning 70, Marques Johnson 56

POST GAME INTERVIEW

At some point in your life you may have to speak into a microphone or be interviewed by a reporter. Most likely, it will be after you have had an outstanding game or made a critical play. The safest approach is to go the cliché route and acknowledge your teammates and the great game plan your coach devised. A more interesting route is to provide some specific insight into why you played so well (Dave was getting me the ball at my favorite spots on the floor, or for some reason they were allowing me to get to the basket all night.) A humble, smiling, relaxed player who can shed some special analysis is golden in the world of the broadcast journalist.

TWITTER WISDOM: "True respect starts with the way you treat others, and it is earned over a lifetime of acting with kindness, honor, and dignity." – Tony Dungy

FEBRUARY 9

BIRTHDAY: Jameer Nelson 82, Phil Ford 56

BEFRIEND THE RIM

Use the rim to protect your shot from getting blocked. When you and your defender are on the same side of the basket a nifty counter is to finish the shot on the opposite side. The rim, net and bottom of the backboard can serve to protect your shot from being blocked. This move can be done from both a standstill or from on the move. Another variation of this concept is to PUT THE DEFENDER IN JAIL. Smart post-up players will try to get as deep into the key as possible especially on ball reversals or when the ball is at the top of the key. When you put your defender in jail, his head ends up directly underneath the net. This makes it very difficult for him to block your shot because the net and rim become obstacles.

TWITTER WISDOM: "You either hate losing enough to change or hate change enough to lose." - @SportsMotto

YOUTUBE ASSIST - The Ultimate Guide to Finishing Around the Rim, "By Any Means Basketball" 6:11

FEBRUARY 10

BIRTHDAY: Josh Jackson 97, Bobby Portis 95, Paul Millsap 85, Tina Thompson 75, John Calipari 59

INJURED OR HURT

Pain happens in basketball. Too many players mistake being momentarily in pain for being injured. Some coaches impose the 3 second rule. You have three seconds to determine if you are hurt or injured. If you are injured, the game will stop and trained personnel will attend to you. If you are merely hurt, you'd better fight through it, pop up and return to the fray in three seconds or you will sit on the bench the rest of the game. Take pride in being tough. Don't desert the troops for even one possession.

TWITTER WISDOM: "Pain can either be destructive or redemptive. We don't get to choose our pain, but we are free to respond to it in any way we choose." - Josh Patrick

FEBRUARY 11

BIRTHDAY: Ben McLemore 93, Nicola Mirotic 91, Hank Gathers 67, James Silas 49

ENCOURAGEMENT AND POSITIVITY

Great teammates are invaluable to any organization. When the work atmosphere rings with a positive vibe, people are more productive. Psychologists, physicians and business experts have documented the phenomenon known as "synergy" (cooperative interaction that exceeds normal expectations). In basketball, loud enthusiastic practices with players shouting encouragement, recognizing hustle plays and constantly slapping hands accelerates team improvement and bonding. Strong team leaders always insist on and generate enthusiasm.

TWITTER WISDOM: "Your ENERGY is everything. Don't tolerate negativity or people that don't appreciate your value! Instead, surround yourself with positive people that bring a great energy to your environment." - Alistair McCaw

YOUTUBE ASSIST - What do Championship Teams Sound Like? "PGC Basketball" 4:09

FEBRUARY 12

BIRTHDAY: Larry Nance, Sr. 59, *Bill Russell 34, *Al Cervi 17

CHART YOUR REPS

Some serious young players find it helpful to keep a record of daily workouts. By charting the number of shots taken and made each day, an aspiring basketball player can accumulate some important data. Perhaps there are places on the floor that seem to be your sweet spots. Shooters will subconsciously gravitate to these spots. Perhaps there are spots that require more focused attention because the angle, background or distance has not been mastered. Another discovery might correspond with the time of the day that you work out. For a variety of reasons including diet, sleep, digestion and our natural bio-rhythms, human bodies respond differently at different points in the day. Having an awareness of when you perform at peak efficiency can inform your physical and mental preparation for games played at unusual hours.

TWITTER WISDOM: "Bad players don't take many things seriously. Average players take games seriously. Good players take games and training seriously. Great players take training, warm-ups, academics, nutrition, weight-room, film study, being a great teammate and games seriously." - @millerstrength

FEBRUARY 13

BIRTHDAY: Luke Ridnour 81, Mike Krzyzewski 47

SUPPORT FRIENDS WHO PLAY OTHER SPORTS

Make it a habit to attend competitions to support your friends or classmates. Students that play less visible sports such as tennis, swimming, lacrosse, field hockey or bowling will appreciate your presence. You are acknowledging their talents and showing respect for their sport. You are also being a wonderful ambassador for your own sport of basketball by recognizing their hard work and their pursuit of competitive excellence. This kind of genuine goodwill breeds unity among competitors.

TWITTER WISDOM: "Helping others is perhaps the greatest joy! You cannot have a perfect day without helping others with no thought of getting something in return." – John Wooden

FEBRUARY 14

BIRTHDAY: Candace Wiggins 87, Richard Hamilton 78, Fred "Mad Dog" Carter, 47, Wali Jones 42

OFF NIGHT ON OFFENSE – ON NIGHT ON DEFENSE

Every player has an off night shooting the ball, however, there are two ends of the floor. Do not allow your shooting woes affect your defensive effort. You simply compound the problem if you sulk and do not bring maximum energy on defense. Disrupting the opponent's offense, pounding the boards, giving quick help and looking to take a charge can often spark a turnover and an easy conversion. Sometimes an easy basket or a trip to the foul line because of an aggressive, attacking defensive play will lift the shooting fog you are in.

TWITTER WISDOM: "Take chances, make mistakes. That's how you grow. Pain nourishes your courage. You have to fail in order to practice being brave." – Mary Tyler Moore

FEBRUARY 15

BIRTHDAY: Mark Price 64

POISE

Poise is the ability to respond with calculation in the heat of pressure and chaos. Poise is a subconsciously rehearsed decision related to relaxation and breath control. A lot of athletes perform well in a group because blame can be shared, but when the game is on the line, and a free throw HAS to be made, only a handful of players relish the glare of the spotlight. Through the years, an athlete must simply build upon small successes. Whether it is hitting the winning shot in a two on two pick-up game, being the last competitor standing in a game of dodge ball or bringing in the winning run with a bloop-single in a little league baseball game, these experiences go into a memory bank to be drawn upon in moments of pressurized expectations. At some point a poised athlete learns to discard the irrational fears of failure and reinterpret the moment as a gift of opportunity to display courage and skill.

TWITTER WISDOM: "Confidence is contagious. So is lack of confidence." – Vince Lombardi

FEBRUARY 16

BIRTHDAY: Herb Williams 86, Kelly Tripucka 59, *Oscar Schmidt 58

OLD FASHION THREE POINT PLAY

Don't avoid the contact. Twisting, fading and bailing out from contact on power moves and layups too often results in empty possessions. Be willing to blast up through the branches and draw the foul. The odds are that you will at least march to the foul line or at most power the ball through the defender and have a chance for a three point play. Drawing contact requires a consistently tough mindset. Sometimes there may be some momentary pain. Enjoy it, shake it off. It confirms your toughness and your willingness to sacrifice for the team. It also places another personal and team foul on your opponent.

TWITTER WISDOM: "TOUGHNESS is • Hard to find• Hard to teach • Hard to beat"" - @SportrsMotto

FEBRUARY 17

BIRTHDAY: Al Harrington 80, *Michael Jordan 63

A TRUE COMPETITOR

A true competitor not only savors the head-on challenge against others, but he is constantly competing with himself. He can never be satisfied with any previous personal achievement. A true competitor is self-critical and demanding of himself; therefore, his coaches never have to demand anything of him. The thrill of competition lies not in gloating over your team's momentary superiority on the scoreboard, it lies in seeking the ideal. A true competitor approaches each game, each practice, each play, and each possession as a chance to seek ultimate personal excellence. To a true competitor, the thrill is in the challenge, the reward is in the effort.

TWITTER WISDOM: "Some people want it to happen, some wish it would happen, others make it happen." – Michael Jordan

YOUTUBE ASSIST – Michael Jordan: The Mind of a Competitor: "Ball is Life" 7:21

FEBRUARY 18

BIRTHDAY: Kentavious Caldwell-Pope 95, Maurice Lucas 52

PRACTICE THREE POINTERS ONE STEP FARTHER OUT

Your practice routine should include a sustained session of shooting 3-pointers from one step farther back from the arc. This practice strengthens your legs, wrists and confidence. When you develop some consistency, the normal distance becomes much more comfortable. Take care to always know your true range. Launching shots from too far out in a game could launch you back onto the bench.

TWITTER WISDOM: "I'm always leery of someone who tells me how hard they work. Hard workers will just work hard and let their results speak for themselves." – Geno Auriemma

YOUTUBE ASSIST - Stephen Curry Shooting Form: Deep Range Secrets, "ShotMechanics" 6:52

FEBRUARY 19

BIRTHDAY: Nicola Jokic 95, Mike Miller 80

ROTTEN APPLE 'WHINE'

Occasionally a sour, negative teammate pollutes the atmosphere. The expression "A rotten apple spoils the whole barrel," has validity. Complainers and whiners drain the positive energy of a team. Constant complainers push the gas pedal while the car is in neutral. There's a lot of noise under the hood, but the car goes nowhere. It's pointless, counterproductive and eventually damages the engine. Open negativity sabotages the team's ultimate goals, creates division and festers like a canker sore. We all succumb to a degree of negativity at one time or another, but learn to recognize when it becomes an annoying habit or a psychological crutch that poisons the group.

TWITTER WISDOM: "The champion-minded distance themselves from excuse makers, energy vampires & doubters. They surround themselves with GREATNESS." Alistair McCaw

FEBRUARY 20

BIRTHDAY: Stephon Marbury 77, *Charles Barkley 63

SMALL SUCCESSES

Small successes are the blocks that form the foundation of self-worth. Little league trophies are the worst kind of sugary candy, a momentary flavor rush that has zero nutritional value. Know what to value. When your shirt is drenched after an hour of holding court in pick-up ball, you know in your heart that "work got done." When you quietly increase the weight on your bench press and your arms quiver on the last two reps, you know in your heart that "work got done." When you step to the line late in a game and your two foul shots pad the lead, you know in your heart that "work got done." Small, meaningful successes collect interest in your memory bank. Small, meaningful successes are the foundational blocks of true self-worth.

TWITTER WISDOM: "Confidence is built with continual, unrelenting effort. It does not precede accomplishment any more than a victory lap precedes the race. Hard work in itself puts the cornerstones of strength and courage firmly in place. Every effort from that point heightens your confidence!" - Ken Mannie

FEBRUARY 21

BIRTHDAY: Steve Francis 77, Paul Westhead 39, Dr. Jack Ramsay 25

SLEEP

Get your rest. Sleep is vastly underrated by athletes. Your body mends, repairs and grows at night. Your brain literally bathes in restorative fluid during deep stages of sleep. Neglecting this aspect of your overall health is foolhardy. Both physical and mental performance are dramatically enhanced by embracing a routine of proper sleep hours. Sleep recharges and calibrates the machine.

HINTS:
1. Establish a routine- bed time –wake-up time
2. Bedroom should be dark and cold like a cave
3. Don't consume caffeine 4 hours before bed
4. Turn off all screens, read words on paper only
5. Don't take naps during the day if you have trouble sleeping at night

TWITTER WISDOM: "If you train hard consistently, eat right, get your sleep, & prioritize your success then you won't need gurus, supplements, or magic drills." - John Cissik

FEBRUARY 22

BIRTHDAY: Rajon Rondo 86, *Julius Irving 50, *Chet Walker 40

POINT GUARD MENTALITY

On all dead-ball situations drift toward your coach to see if he needs to converse. He may want to run a special play or switch defenses. He may need you to tell teammates to switch the men they are guarding or to mention something to the referee. During foul shots make sure that everyone knows who they are guarding and that everyone is on the same page both offensively and defensively. Point guards should also bark out reminders to block out, to watch-out for the press or to check the time on the clock.

Point guards must never be denied an in-bounds pass when guarded by one man. Pop loose by crowding and freezing the defender on your body then knife quickly to open spaces giving a hand target to the in-bounder. Also, a quick dart along the baseline between the defender and the in-bounder can result in a safe pass.

Point guards are floor generals. Demand the ball from teammates with two definitive hand-claps. These claps can be heard in the top row of any arena.

The point guard is responsible for starting the offense close enough to the basket so that there is proper spacing, and he/she must always be aware of getting back on defense. When a point guard penetrates, an off-guard should always circle back to the top of the key so that someone is back on defense.

Point guards must be an extension of the coach out on the floor.

FEBRUARY 23

BIRTHDAY: Jamal Murray 97, D'Angelo Russell 96, Andrew Wiggins 95, Jia Perkins 82

COMPLIMENT YOUR TEAMMATES

Compliments are the highest octane fuel known to humans. A quiet, sincere compliment delivered at the right moment can linger for days and be remembered for a lifetime. Affirming a teammate's on-court contributions, practice habits or personality create bonds of unity. Everyone loves to hear words of respect and recognition. Render compliments freely and without expectation of reciprocation.

TWITTER WISDOM: "Good people are happy when something good happens to someone else." – Dean Smith

FEBRUARY 24

BIRTHDAY: Eddie Johnson 55

PRESSURE

Life is like a rubber band. If there is not enough tension, we live in a loose state of pointless inaction. If there's too much tension, something will snap. But if there is just the right range of tension, we thrive in a safely balanced world of goals and challenges. In the grand scheme of things, basketball pressure is a joke. Try living in a war-torn, bombed-out village in a state of constant hunger and fear, and your missed foul shot last Friday will seem embarrassingly trivial. Sports are designed to create artificial pressure that will test our level of skill and poise - no more, no less. The first step in being able to handle pressure is to reduce the imaginary and exaggerated consequences attached to it. The second step is to enter the contest convinced that you did every-thing in your power to be ready for the moment, because in reality YOU ONLY FEEL PRESSURE WHEN YOU'RE UNPREPARED.

TWITTER WISDOM: "Pressure is nothing more than the shadow of great opportunity." – Michael Johnson

FEBRUARY 25

BIRTHDAY: Thon Maker 97, Jimmer Fredette 89, Joakim Noah 85, Kurt Rambis 58, Cincinnatus Powell 42

PRACTICE THE RARE-OCCASION SHOT

You never know when you might end up with the ball at the end of a quarter or game and need to heave a ¾ or ½ court shot. Players should occasionally practice these shots just to gage the required strength and arc necessary. Also, a normal shot release cannot be taken under .3 seconds, so only a volleyball setting motion or a tap-in is legal.

Once in a great while, a player will need to purposely miss a free throw in the waning seconds in order to give his team a chance to win. There is a correct method to insure the highest chance of success. Too many times a player will shoot the ball too hard off the board and the ball does not hit the rim. Also, players often accidentally bank the ball into the basket wiping out a chance to win. Finally, many players will step across the line before the ball hits the rim trying to retrieve their own miss.

The best-practice is as follows: 1. Release the ball without going through your free throw ritual as soon as the referee tosses you the ball. It may catch an opponent off-guard. DO NOT RUSH THE SHOT. 2. Aim for a spot on the backboard slightly right or left of center so it careens off the board and then bounces off the edge of the rim. Hopefully the ball pops into the center of the lane where alert teammates can keep the play alive.

TWITTER WISDOM: "Luck is when preparation meets opportunity." – Seneca

FEBRUARY 26

BIRTHDAY: Steve Blake 80, Rolando Blackman 59, Bingo Smith 46

GETTING BACK ON DEFENSE

Transitioning from offense to defense is perhaps the most under-emphasized fundamental of team basketball. The first two steps of direction-change are critical to preventing easy baskets down court. If your first two steps are lazy, nonchalant jogs then a hustling opponent could gain an advantage further down the court. Allowing opponents to beat you down the court is unforgiveable especially if it could have been prevented by two quicker, purposeful strides at the beginning of the transition. Successful fast break layups are a combination of a hustling offense as well as a lax sense of defensive urgency. All fast break layups can be prevented if a team is committed to getting back and having the numbers advantage near their opponent's hoop.

TWITTER WISDOM: "A WINNER does the dirty work... not because they like the dirty work but because they love WINNING!" @ RandyEdsall

FEBRUARY 27

BIRTHDAY: Devin Harris 83, *James Worthy 61

POSITIVE SELF-TALK

Positive self-talk in athletes improves performance. It sounds simple but it is difficult to implement because our inner dialogue is often bombarded by negative thoughts of past failures. Even well-meaning adults can reinforce our insecurities through judgmental and insensitive comments. How does an athlete replace these negative messages with self-initiated positivity?

Create a mantra – a repeatable phrase that plants a successful mindset. Choose something as simple as "This is going in!" every time you step to the line or "I've done this before."

Access a vivid visual of success - pull a success video from your memory files. See yourself performing the skill in living color on the movie screen of your memory. True belief becomes entrenched and transfers to performance.

Other terms for this technique are 'guided imagery,' 'mental rehearsal,' or 'stepping into the feeling.' Remember that self-talk must be practiced. Incorporate it into your year-round training.

TWITTER WISDOM: "If you let outside noise affect you, then it means you value their opinion more than you value your own opinion." – Chip Kelly

FEBRUARY 28

BIRTHDAY: Tayshaun Prince 80, Adrian Dantley 56, Sylvia Hatchell 52, Dean Smith 31

PASS ON YOUR KNOWLEDGE

Players on organized school teams will probably have a chance to work camps or clinics for younger players. Be flattered that you have a chance to impact the development of younger players. Run your station or drill with enthusiasm. Share your current expertise. Make helpful corrections and invest your energy into the art and craft of teaching. Standing around with bored indifference is the posture of a loser. Plunge in, sell out and give the kids a meaningful piece of yourself. Pass on your knowledge to these eager young ballers.

TWITTER WISDOM: "Be the best version of yourself. Have passion, a great attitude, a single-minded focus, relentless energy, and always finish." – Jason Garrett

FEBRUARY (29)

BIRTHDAY: Chucky Brown 68,

WHO SHOULD TAKE THE LAST SHOT IN A CLOSE GAME?

The best player. PERIOD. No decoys, No discussion.

OPTION B – (See above)

TWITTER WISDOM: "Bad Shooters are always open, it's called Scouting...don't take the shot the Defense wants us to take, work to get the shot we want, it's called discipline." - Don Meyer

YOUTUBE ASSIST – Best Game Winners of NBA History, "Rcod 22" 7:04

MARCH 1

BIRTHDAY: Chris Webber 73, Yolanda Griffith 70, Brian Winters 52

THE CHAMPIONSHIP HOURS

Fall in love with the process of getting better at the game. There is something intoxicating about waking up to another day of personal improvement. The championship hours are between 5 a.m. and 7 a.m. Rising before 95% of your opponents and running over the hills while the moon is still visible or slipping into the weight room with a handful of hard-core teammates before daylight can be exhilarating. Dedicating your life to the pursuit of a dream breeds discipline and toughness. Attacking the day with purpose and commitment clarifies your identity. Instead of growing randomly like a weed, nurture and prune your life like a rose.

TWITTER WISDOM: "My goal in the off-season is to create the best athlete I can create and give it to the coaches and say here, use it how you want." – J. J. Watt

YOUTUBE ASSIST: Welcome To The Grind - Sports Motivational Video, "Jerry Dobson" 3:26de

MARCH 2

BIRTHDAY: Jason Smith 86, *Dejan Bodiroga 73, Clair Bee 1896

SEEK OUT THE BEST COMPETITION

Young players should seek challenges. Find the courts that attract the best players and show up during the prime hours. Never be afraid of being humiliated by an older, better player. Be eager to take the toughest defensive assignment in a pick-up game. In the off-season, your quickest acceleration in improvement comes from testing yourself time and time again. Slow footed post players should try to guard a "water-bug" point guard. Just give him a little more cushion and bother him with your length when he shoots. Little guys should guard a post once in a while. Get a taste of what it's like down in the trench-paint. Evaluate, adjust and find a way to 'get it done.' You might get burnt a few times, but you are stretching your skill and knowledge of the game.

TWITTER WISDOM: "The only thing even in this world is the number of hours in a day. The difference in winning or losing is what you do with those hours." – Woody Hayes

MARCH 3

BIRTHDAY: Jason Tatum 98, Erika de Sousa 82, Willie Wise 47

THE POWER OF SMILING

Smiling produces a chemical reaction in the brain that releases endorphins. Smiling relaxes the body and reduces tension. Smiling can be a unique strategy when you are placed in a pressure situation like stepping to the line to shoot a crucial free throw at the end of a game. Smiling conveys confidence, control and perspective. You will be amazed at the transformational qualities linked to smiling. Tap into the power of the smile.

TWITTER WISDOM: "A group becomes a team when each member is sure enough of himself and his contributions to praise the skills of the others." – Norman Shidle

MARCH 4

BIRTHDAY: Jared Sullinger 92, Draymond Green 90, Kevin Johnson 66

HOW TO DRAW A FOUL

Some players have a knack for getting to the line. This talent brings multiple benefits. First of all the shots are free and your scoring average gets padded. Secondly, you have put an opponent one step closer to disqualification. Thirdly, your team is getting closer to the bonus limit for automatic two shot fouls. Fourthly, if your team is behind late in a game, you have stopped the clock to allow substitutions and better full-court pressing opportunities.

Aggressive penetrators who invite contact and know how to shield their body against potential shot blockers are always marching to the line. Anytime that a head fake gets a defender in the air, they are prime fodder for the shooter. Just go up through them as they return to earth. Referees invariably call the foul. Of course some drama-class exaggeration can influence a referee. Dribblers who get bumped often throw their head back in whiplash, or players powering in a layup through defenders will bellow out a painful grown to trigger a foul call. Another slick trick while advancing the ball against a pressuring defender is to beat him with a dribble burst then slant in and suddenly slow down so the defender stumbles into your back. Some exaggeration helps to sell it. Make the refs blow their whistles.

TWITTER WISDOM: "Experience is a hard teacher because she gives the test first, the lesson afterward." – Vernon Law

YOUTUBE ASSIST – How to Draw Fouls like James Harden, "By Any Means Basketball" 4:20

MARCH 5

BIRTHDAY: Mason Plumley 90, Corey Brewer 86, Wally Sczcerbiak 77, Scott Skiles 64

WHO ARE YOU WHEN NOBODY'S LOOKING?

The ultimate test of your character is the choices you make when nobody is looking and you think you won't get caught. It's easy to do the right thing when a cop is around, but each time you compromise your moral values you weaken your self-worth. Self-betrayal has a noxious smell about it. Players who stop doing a drill when the coach's back is turned are always caught. Plagiarizing a paper, cheating, stealing or spreading malicious gossip may provide some temporary short cuts and satisfaction, but each act becomes a termite that eats away at your moral foundation. No human has ever resisted every temptation, but don't fall into the habit of rationalizing and making excuses for words and actions that you instinctively know are wrong.

TWITTER WISDOM: "The grade is easy, when it comes to integrity. It's either '100' percent or '0' percent. It's an easy grading scale on that one." - Jim Harbaugh

MARCH 6

BIRTHDAY: Marcus Smart 94, Michael Finley 73, *Shaquille O'Neill 72, Eric "Sleepy" Floyd 60

FUEL FOR THE ENGINE

You cannot outwork a bad diet. You will not encounter your peak performance if you do not pay attention to what you are (and are not) putting into your body. Consider your body a Ferrari, not a golf cart. Use only the highest grade of fuel. When it comes to nutrition, if it comes from the earth, it's good for you. There are no Pepsi rivers or Skittle trees so avoid those foods. Keep it simple.

TWITTER WISDOM: "The food you eat can either be the safest and most powerful form of medicine or the slowest form of poison!" Kyle Gilbert

MARCH 7

BIRTHDAY: Ian Clark 91, *Andy Phillip 22

ECONOMY OF MOTION

Watch the fluid movement of a great sprinter. There is no head-wagging or flailing of arms, just a streamlined machine moving in effortless flight down the track. Watch a great baseball hitter. A tight compact swing allows for faster bat speed and more time to see the pitch. The great boxing champion Joe Louis claimed that he knocked out opponents with a six-inch punch, no wind-up and no telegraphing.

Strong two-handed rebounders rarely have the ball popped out of their hands, as opposed to one-handed 'stetchers' who expose the ball as they gather it in. Good shooters eliminate wasted motion. A simple, replicable shooting form produces more opportunity for consistency. Players with long sweeps of the ball from their waist to above or behind their head are rarely accurate shooters. Players that take the ball across their body or face are rarely accurate shooters. Players that directly lift the ball to their shooting pocket then release the ball at a comfortable height according to their strength, have the best chance of becoming accurate shooters. Streamline your movement for maximum efficiency.

TWITTER WISDOM: "Less is more." – Robert Browning

MARCH 8

BIRTHDAY: Moriah Jefferson 94, Kenny Smith 65, Buck Williams 60

THE DISCIPLINE OF DISCIPLINE

Discipline is simply making yourself do what you DON'T want to do. Discipline is the common denominator found in every successful enterprise. Great competitors embrace repetition and sacrifice, but by adopting the "habit of attack" in their daily work, they enter a second level of mental preparation called the DISCIPLINE OF DISCIPLINE. It's not enough to just complete a workout, but one should muster a daily determination to attack the workout. This requires a deeper reserve of discipline that scrapes away all the excuses and negativity in order to maximize the day's efforts. Get your mind and heart into the highest gear to reap the full benefit of each day's work

TWITTER WISDOM: "I run on the road long before I dance under the lights." – Muhammad Ali

MARCH 9

BIRTHDAY: Matt Barnes 80, Mahmoud Abdul-Rauf 69

PRACTICE AGAINST HOLOGRAMS

When your skill level becomes sophisticated enough, try to structure your workouts to incorporate layers of mental anticipation. This is called the "Hologram" workout. After the initial move, you will imagine a second and perhaps a third defender who will appear to you like a hologram coming at you from the help side. Of course the defender won't be there in physical reality, but you will anticipate defensive help and immediately react to these imaginary obstacles by a spin dribble, a hesitation move, a subtle glance at the rim, a burst of speed or a knifing change of direction. Be creative and practice at 'game speed' and 'game envisioned.'

TWITTER WISDOM: "When you catch a glimpse of your potential, that's when passion is born." – Zig Ziglar

MARCH 10

BIRTHDAY: Zach Levine 95, Austin Carr 48, Jim Valvano 46, Marques Haynes 26

FINAL SECONDS PUSH

Did you know that a skilled and fairly quick dribbler can cover the full length of a basketball court in four dribbles? When an opponent hits what seems to be a winning shot from under ten seconds down to four seconds, instead of calling a time-out the best strategy is to quickly in-bounds the ball and PUSH IT UP THE COURT as quickly as possible. Very often the opposing team is in celebration mode, and they are petrified of fouling the dribbler which provides an open path to a great shot. Go coast to coast on a non-stop supersonic flight.

TWITTER WISDOM: "If you have dedicated players who believe in themselves, you don't need a lot of talent." – Paul 'Bear' Bryant

MARCH 11

BIRTHDAY: Anthony Davis 93, Elton Brand 79, Becky Hammon 77

DRAG THE POST DOUBLE-TEAM AWAY FROM THE BASKET

Effective post players are often quickly double teamed by the nearest defender. The open or unguarded offensive player should immediately dive to the basket for a quick-hitting layup. If this pass is not available, the double-teamed post-player should take a quick dribble or two away from the basket to drag the defenders with him/her. This creates more passing space and a greater distance for the defense to recover. A quick two pass swing of the ball to the opposite side of the court creates opportunities for free-lance penetration or kicks to open shooters.

TWITTER WISDOM: "If you don't feel you have something to prove every day, you'll never improve." – Billy Donovan

MARCH 12

BIRTHDAY: Jerami Grant 94, Shea Ralph 78, Isaiah rider 71, *Bob Houbregs 32

MINDFULNESS

Mindfulness is the basic human ability to be fully present, aware of where you are and what you are doing, and not to be overly reactive or overwhelmed by what's going on around you. Some players have an uncanny sense of calm about them. They seem to ignore the chaos swirling around them and compete with an unflappable demeanor. How are these chosen few able to overcome the multiple distractions that plague normal players such as physical opponents, a screaming coach, rude fans, inconsistent referees, temperamental teammates or a slippery floor? Perhaps they have cultivated an inner awareness through self-talk or reflection. Phil Jackson, perhaps the greatest basketball coach of the 20th century encouraged mindfulness through self-hypnosis, meditation and group visualization. He wanted his players to develop an intuitive feel for how their movements and those of everyone else on the floor were interconnected. No wonder he was referred to as the ZEN MASTER.

TWITTER WISDOM: "My confidence grew out of knowing that when the spirit was right and the players were attuned to one another, the game was likely to unfold in our favor." – Phil Jackson

MARCH 13

BIRTHDAY: Tristan Thompson 91, Caron Butler 80, Cliff Robinson 60

FRENEMIES

frenemy: N. (origin- **MEAN GIRLS** movie) *Someone who is both friend and enemy, a relationship that can be both mutually beneficial and harmful. Someone who may act as your friend while having alterior motives.* Urban Dictionary.

Relationships are complex. As one grows up, groups of friends can change dramatically. Childhood playmates often drift into different social circles. A sport's team brings together a variety of personalities. The most successful teams blend these personalities and share a set of values and goals that always focus on daily improvement; however, friction will undoubtedly rear its ugly head over the course of a season. Teams with strong leaders never allow any jealousy, ill-will or friction to spill over onto the playing floor. Try not to fall into the "frenemy" category. Monitor the way you speak about teammates when they are not present. Leave no room for misinterpretation. Regaining a teammate's trust is nearly impossible once he/she feels betrayed.

TWITTER WISDOM: "All kids need is a little help, a little hope and somebody who believes in them." – Magic Johnson

MARCH 14

BIRTHDAY: Marvin Bagley 99, Patrick Patterson 89, Steph Curry 88, Wes Unseld 46, Kay Yow 42

SLAP BALL OFF KNEE

Very, very few basketball players can cleanly block a shot from behind. The best strategy for preventing a break-away layup is to catch the dribbler as he/she momentarily slows down to elevate toward the rim. All players must bring the ball to their waist, and this is the perfect time to slap the ball off their knee as they jump vertically toward the rim. Not only is the layup prevented, but there is also a chance that the possession goes in your favor. Never underestimate how quickly you can close-in on a break-away dribbler. Even if you commit a foul, the player will have to earn two points from 15 feet away instead of an easy 2 point layup. Always chase down the dribbler like it's the last bus of the night.

TWITTER WISDOM: "You cannot allow the score of the ball game to dictate your intensity." – Jeff Brantley

YOUTUBE ASSIST – 3 Sneaky Tricks TO GET MORE STEALS with Coach Damin Altizer, "EGTBasketball" 5:53

MARCH 15

BIRTHDAY: Jabari Parker 95, Terry Cummings 61

THE QUICK-LIFT

When you find yourself with the ball on either side of the basket guarded by one player, the tendency is to head fake in a predictable rhythm before releasing the ball. Smart inside defenders learn to time your release; however, very often the defender does not have his arms fully extended. Instead, one hand may be lightly touching your body while the other is held in half-extension in order to help with his thrust when he jumps. An effective skill is to freeze the defender with a nanosecond of hesitation then blast the ball into shooting position before the defender can get his arm up to block it. Concentrating on the speed of the lift-to-shooting-position before the player can react, regularly results in a successful basket. Players should practice "quick-lifting" the ball from their waste to above their heads to get a sense of the core-strength and fast-twitch arm muscle required to out-quick the reaction time of the defender.

TWITTER WISDOM: "What are you doing today to beat yesterday?" – @SportsMotto

MARCH 16

BIRTHDAY: Joel Embid 94, Tim Hardaway Jr. 92, Blake Griffin 89, C. Vivian Stringer 48

SOCCER IN-BOUNDS PASS

If an in-bounder is being pressured whether from the baseline or sideline, a soccer style pass is always the safest. After a score by an opponent, the in-bounder should never flip the ball with one hand to a teammate because the passing hand can't be retracted when a crafty opponent surprises and ambushes the receiver. Also, the in-bounder on an out-of-bounds play from under his own basket should use a soccer style inbounds in order to prevent a tipped pass. Throwing the ball from the hip creates a sharp trajectory. Throwing the ball with two hands from head-level eliminates the dangerous deflection area.

TWITTER WISDOM: "You must strength train in order to increase the capacity of your muscle fibers and maximize the rate of muscular force production." @VoltAthletics

MARCH 17

BIRTHDAY: Terry Rozier 94, Kyle Korver 81, Danny Ainge 59, Willie Somerset 42

MOVING WITHOUT THE BALL

Guarding the dribbler is relatively easy because you just move your feet and keep the ball in front of you. Guarding a player who knows how to move without the ball can be a nightmare. A player with instincts to run a give-and-go, to sucker a defender into a back door cut, to slip a screen or to curl around or flare off a screen for a jump shot is far more dangerous than the ball-pounding dribbler. Off-guards who know how to read penetration and float to the sight-lines of the driver will receive numerous opportunities for open shots. Constant movement can wear down the will of your defender. Late in the game, scoring opportunities occur that had previously been defended.

TWITTER WISDOM: "Recovery is probably the most important and most overlooked component of physical development." @voltathletics

YOUTUBE ASSIST: Klay Thompson – Off Ball Movement 16/17: "Evan Gualberto" 11:37

MARCH 18

BIRTHDAY: Skal Labissiere 96, Brian Scalabrine 78, Jeff Mulllins 42

PLAYING WHILE SICK

Never risk your over-all health. Obey all doctor's orders. If physical exertion can exacerbate your condition then do NOT play. There are times, however, when athletes can push through some minor fever or cold symptoms and perform admirably. Michael Jordan and Roberto Clemente were two athletes who performed impeccably when they were 'under the weather.' Sometimes being a little bit sick makes the athlete focus more on the execution of fundamentals. It can also take the edge off the pressure to excel because there is a built-in excuse if the performance is subpar. Immediate hydration and rest should be a part of every recovery strategy.

TWITTER WISDOM: "Toughness is in the soul and spirit, not in muscles or an immature mind." - Alex Karras

MARCH 19

BIRTHDAY: Andre Miller 76, Scott May 54

TACTILE BONDING

High fives, low fives, hand-slaps, fist bumps, chest bumps, pulling a teammate up from the floor and bench arm-locking inspire energy and create team bonding. These demonstrations of connection are critically important to team morale. When every player is as happy for the success of their teammates as they are for their own success, a special esprit-de-corps flows through the team. Be first and be generous with these outward shows of camaraderie and respect. Few things in life are more fulfilling than being part of close-knit group of athletes.

TWITTER WISDOM: "Culture will beat scheme every day." – Chip Kelly

MARCH 20

BIRTHDAY: Michelle Snow 80, Jamal Crawford 80, Mookie Blaylock 67, Pat Riley 45

BUILD A WALL

When the man you are guarding has you trapped near the basket with the ball, your immediate instinct should be to build a wall. Brace solidly against his body with both arms raised directly above your head. Two good things can result: 1. The player gets discouraged from shooting because of the looming obstacle of your arms and the intense lower body pressure. 2. The shot accuracy is affected by the shooter crashing into the strong, stationary barrier of your body. In addition, you avoid drawing a foul by foolishly hopping into the air to try to block the shot, and you are in a much better position to rebound a missed shot.

TWITTER WISDOM: "Danger for most lies not in setting our aim too high and falling short; but in setting our aim too low and achieving our mark." – Michaelangelo

MARCH 21

BIRTHDAY: Darius Miller 90, Scott Williams 68, Mike Dunleavy 54

EARLY LEAD DECEPTION

Never, never be deceived by an early lead. Whether your team is ahead or behind on the score board, there is a psychological danger associated with the optics of these early numbers. A sense of false confidence or a mindset of desperation can erode the implementation of a solid game plan. Shooting percentages almost always stabilize. The hot team cools, and the cold team puts together a meaningful run. Part of the beauty of sports is the roller coaster ride of momentum.

TWITTER WISDOM: "I think that it's perhaps harder to learn from victory than it is from defeat." – Bobby Knight

MARCH 22

BIRTHDAY: Taurean Prince 94, Marcus Camby 74, Shawn Bradley 72, *Ed Macauley 28

SHOOTING AND BODY AWARENESS

Shooting hundreds of shots off the "gun"/ ball rack or from a person who is rebounding for you certainly aids muscle memory, but you should incorporate movement to simulate real game situations. Receiving a pass coming off a screen from the left or right requires two different motions to square up to the basket. Popping out to either corner from the block requires two different pivots in order to shoot. Flaring away from a passer, drifting to a sight-line of a penetrator, stepping into a shot thrown out to the perimeter by an offensive rebounder or shooting the ball off the dribble each presents a different set of body mechanics. To precisely calculate the geometry of a successful shot, a good shooter's body must be educated to respond to the multiple angles and shifts in body momentum. Shot opportunities in a basketball game involve a range of circumstances that should be consciously practiced. Add 'situation shooting' to your 'spot shooting' drills. Basketball is not a game of darts.

TWITTER WISDOM: "We don't rise to the level of our expectations, we fall to the level of our training." Archilochos

MARCH 23

BIRTHDAY: Andrew Wiggins 95, Kyrie Irving 92, Gordon Hayward 90, Jason Kidd 73, Moses Malone 55, Ann Meyers 55, Geno Auriemma 54

TAP-INS

Tapping in an offensive rebound for a score is an invaluable skill that is rarely taught or practiced. Players with natural talent will tap in an errant shot because of their timing, coordination and jumping ability, but paying attention to a few simple fundamentals can help an average athlete be more effective with this skill. First of all an offensive rebounder needs to recognize when a rebound is primed for a 'tap-in.' Some rebounds are heavy and bounce high and deep, others are light and hover near the cylinder. The light rebounds near the cylinder are perfect for a tap-in. Players should stiffen their arms, flatten their palms and poke the ball deftly with their fingertips. Quick recognition and quick jumping provide the advantage. Sometimes two or three taps in succession can be accomplished because of positioning and determination. This skill can be practiced against a wall or on a backboard.

TWITTER WISDOM: "Unmotivated people gravitate toward other unmotivated people because they love to remind each other why it's everyone else's fault." - Bob Shipley

MARCH 24

BIRTHDAY: Miles Turner 96, Chris Bosh 84

STEAL THE DRIBBLE

Only a chosen few should work on this skill because unless you are blessed with unnatural quickness or some unusually long arms, you will most likely commit a senseless foul; however, there are a few tips that are worth considering. As you slide up the floor closely guarding the dribbler, try to time your swoop the moment the ball hits the floor. This gives you a definite reference point for when the ball is the farthest from his palm. Also, the most vulnerable time for the dribbler is when his attention is locked-in trying to locate a teammate which is often as he crosses half court. Also, if you time his cross-over dribble with an opposite swipe of your hand, you can sometimes knock the ball off of his knee. The ball is at its closest point to you when he switches hands in front of his body. Be crafty, but also be selective in your attempts at thievery.

TWITTER WISDOM: "I love it when people doubt me. It makes me work harder to prove them wrong." – Derek Jeter

MARCH 25

BIRTHDAY: T.J. McConnell 92, Marco Belinelli 86, Kyle Lowry 86, Sheryl Swoopes 71, Avery Johnson 65

BABY HOOK

The 'baby hook' or 'half hook' is a weapon that should be in every big man's tool kit. Unlike the old-fashion, fully extended sweeping hook of yesteryear, the baby hook is an efficient adaptation. The baby hook retains the same sideways turn of the shoulder to shield the ball from the defender, but the release point of the ball is higher and closer to the head. A quick jump off of two feet and a simultaneous soft loft of the ball creates a floater that is difficult to time or block. If you become adept with both hands, your inside effectiveness becomes lethal.

TWITTER WISDOM: "Mental toughness is when you can find fuel in an empty tank." @sports motto

MARCH 26

BIRTHDAY: Justise Winslow 96, John Stockton 62, Wayne Embry 37

THE DISEASE OF ME

True humility not only comes from recognizing and admitting our personal flaws and fallibilities, but from acknowledging the rights, concerns and special gifts of others. Nothing damages a team more than selfishness, otherwise known as the "disease of me." Players who obsess over statistics – how many shots they get, how many points they score, how many times their play is called – are directly interfering with the ONLY stat that matters – the final score. If a team commits to the lofty standards of hustle, humility and harmony; they are most likely inoculated from the "disease of me."

TWITTER WISDOM: "I" loses games. @sportsmotto

MARCH 27

BIRTHDAY: Chris Loften 86, Danny Fortson 76, Ed Pinckney 63

SAVING THE BALL

When you are saving the ball under your opponent's basket, NEVER throw it toward the hoop. It often ends up as a "fool's assist." Have the presence of mind to flip it toward the wing or farther down court. When one of your teammates is saving a ball from going out of bounds, rush to a place where he/she can either see you or he can hear his first name being called (opponents rarely know first names). The flicker of your movement and uniform color might catch his/her peripheral vision. In other words don't just be a stationary spectator watching to see if your teammate successfully reaches the ball.

TWITTER WISDOM: "The Six W's: Work Will Win When Wishing Won't." – Todd Blackledge

MARCH 28

BIRTHDAY: Jordan McRae 91, Luke Walton 80, Byron Scott 61, *Rick Barry 44, *Jerry Sloan 42

MEMORY VISION

Great passers do not have eyes in the back of their heads, but they may have cameras or a GPS device. The movement of players is fluid especially on a fast break and a player with memory vision makes quick and detailed notes of the location, speed and ETA (estimated time of arrival) of his teammates as well as the opposition. Just sensing that a teammate is filling a lane and dropping a soft assist comes from both a great sense of peripheral and memory vision. Penetrators who leave their feet but are effectively blocked must sometimes throw "hope passes" to players they hope are where they imagine them to be. No look passes and spectacular "saves" of balls that land safely in the hands of teammates are products of "memory vision."

TWITTER WISDOM: "Come into practice every day with the mindset of wanting to learn, wanting to get better." - Sue Bird

YOUTUBE ASSIST – Magic Johnson Top 32 Assists of Career, "NBA Reel" 5:19

MARCH 29

BIRTHDAY: *Walt "Clyde" Frazier

LEAVING YOUR FEET

Don't be a flopping fish that leaps at every head or shot fake. The rule of thumb is to stay on your feet until your opponent leaves his. Jump second. Once you are in the air you are suspended and helpless, vulnerable to fouling and to every other indignity of defensive exploitation. It's tempting to try to swat every shot you can, but you are being supremely undisciplined and hurting your team. Sometimes the best thing to happen early in a game is to have your own shot blocked, because from that point on your defender will be hopping like a frog on a hot skillet every time you shot-fake. Also, don't make a habit of jumping in the air to throw passes. Your hang time dictates your decision time and for most players that's measured in nanoseconds.

TWITTER WISDOM: "Don't be afraid to fail. Experience is just mistakes you don't make anymore." – Joe Garagiola

YOUTUBE ASSIST – NBA Best Fakes, "Hoops Card" 4:20

MARCH 30

BIRTHDAY: *Jerry Lucas 40

PLAYING WITH FOUL TROUBLE

Most coaches will immediately bench key players who are in foul trouble in order to minimize their chances of being disqualified. Occasionally, a player is irreplaceable and their absence would lead to certain team defeat. If forced to play with foul trouble, aggressive players must now fight against their nature on both ends of the court. A player in foul trouble must consciously remind himself to be absolutely disciplined by avoiding the following impulses: 1. Reaching-in on a dribbler. 2. Jumping to block shots. 3. Rebounding over the back of an opponent. 4. Setting a questionable screen. 5. Leaving his/her feet to pass on penetration. 6. Taking risky charges 7. Slapping at the ball to strip a rebounder of the ball. Players in foul trouble will also become a prime target of the opposition. Teams will purposely attack them by isolating them on the wing and driving right at them, backscreening and flopping for a charge or posting them up on the block where contact is inevitable. When you are forced to play with foul trouble sometimes it is smart to lose an occasional personal battle.

TWITTER WISDOM: "Others can stop you temporarily. You are the only one who can do it permanently." – Zig Ziglar

MARCH 31

BIRTHDAY: DeAndre Liggins 88, Steve Smith 69, J.R. Reid 68

SIBLINGS

Your family is your first and most important team. How you treat your siblings sheds light on your potential as a teammate. Literally being a blood brother or sister, or being part of a blended family creates and demands loyalty. Long after your playing days are over, you will be connected to those who shared your journey to adulthood. Life can be filled with landmines and obstacles that require temporary support from family members. Younger siblings can be annoying and obnoxious, older siblings can be bossy and condescending. As hard as it may seem, strive to be considerate, thoughtful, patient and respectful. Don't fall into the toxic trap of selfish bickering and daily resentment. Someday you will need each other.

TWITTER WISDOM: "I follow three rules: Do the right thing, do the best you can, and always show people you care." – Lou Holtz

APRIL 1

BIRTHDAY: Brook and Robin Lopez 88, Tangela Smith 77, Mark Jackson 65, Kevin Duckworth 64, Norm Van Lier 47

THE BALL FINDS HUSTLE

"The ball finds hustle," is a unique way to phrase a universal sports truth. The player whose motor is always in turbo gear seems to get his hands on the ball in so many different situations – deflections, rebounds, tap-ins, loose balls, saves and fast-break layups. A team that is stacked with hungry, hustling, proud and strong-willed players is very difficult to defeat. The ball just seems attracted to those guys and always ends up in their arms.

TWITTER WISDOM: "I played the game one way. I gave it everything I had. It doesn't take any ability to hustle." – Wade Boggs

YOUTUBE ASSIST – NBA Top 10 Hustle Plays of All Time, "Dunk Buster" 3:30

APRIL 2

BIRTHDAY: Larry Drew 68, Jim McDaniels 58

RESPECT THE GAME

Some tactics are not in the spirit of the game. Stepping to the foul line to shoot free throws for another player is wrong. Occasionally, a foul is called during a scramble for a loose ball and the referee is preoccupied with identifying the person who committed the foul and reporting it to the scorer's table. The deception of replacing the rightful shooter with a better shooter is not clever, it's immoral. Do not rationalize the action by claiming that the referees are responsible for getting it right. You disrespect the game with this behavior.

Also, some players believe they have the right to sweep their elbows into the face of a crowding defender claiming they have a right to that space. Loosening an opponent's teeth or fracturing their cheekbone is not only disrespecting the game but is the naked action of a coward.

TWITTER WISDOM: "What is right is more important than who is right." – John Wooden

APRIL 3

BIRTHDAY: Frank Mason 94, "Never Nervous" Pervis Ellison 67, *Earl Lloyd 28

DON'T GET BACK-TAPPED

Defensive players often allow a dribbler to slide past them then reach around to tap the ball away. Alert ball-handlers should never allow this to happen. After losing the ball a few times in this manner, an evolving dribbler will always sense the trick coming. As soon as you feel the defender in range of attempting this kind of steal, the next dribble should be centered in front of your body. This simple maneuver takes the ball out of range of the back-tapper and creates a 5 on 4 advantage. Make the defender pay for attempting this lazy, cheap and risky tactic.

TWITTER WISDOM: "Progress is rarely a straight line." - @CoachMotto

APRIL 4

BIRTHDAY: Frank Kaminsky 93, Ben Gordon 83, Larry Miller 46, Bill Bridges 39

CREATE SOME CHAOS

In his personal shooting workout, Ray Allen, one of the greatest shooters in the history of the NBA, would occasionally simulate brief scenarios of chaos. He would either kneel or lie flat on his back then scramble up as the ball was thrown to him for a shot. He wanted to give his body some familiarity with the rare but possible situation for when he was knocked down or tripped. Another "chaos" shooting drill is to have two balls thrown at you simultaneously from two angles exposing the mind to an unexpected distraction forcing extreme concentration and quick reaction.

TWITTER WISDOM: "If your daily routine looks like everyone else's, the results will be average. Excellence demands different." - Brian Early

APRIL 5

BIRTHDAY: Justin Holiday 89, Stephen Jackson 78

PICK UP THE LOOSE BALL

When a ball is popped loose, the player who reaches it first often tries to regain control by dribbling it even though hustling opponents are hotly pursuing it as well. What often happens is the ball gets poked and is loose again. The first person to the ball should always jump-stop and secure it before putting it back down as a dribble. This eliminates the risk of an unseen opponent ambushing the recovery from the player's blind spots.

TWITTER WISDOM: "There is a common misconception that you have to be on the court to help your team. Playing time does not determine your impact on your team." – Cassidy Lichtman

APRIL 6

BIRTHDAY: Spencer Dinwiddie 93, Bison Dele 69, John Shumate 69

PRIDE

Your signature is on everything you do, so make sure it reflects the pride that you have in yourself. How you dress, how you talk, how you compete, and how you live will determine how you are remembered. When pride is channeled for positive goals, then greatness is attainable. Pride is a sense of achievement, worth, approval and connection. When an athlete reaches down inside himself to find that 'something extra' that he is not absolutely sure is there, he taps into a mystical world of self-understanding and tastes the ripening fruit of his/her hard work.

TWITTER WISDOM: "Win or lose you will never regret working hard, making sacrifices, being disciplined, or focusing too much. Success is measured by what we have done to prepare for competition." – John Walton Smith

APRIL 7

BIRTHDAY: Thurl Bailey 61, Bo Lamar 51

CHEAT STEP BACKWARDS

Whenever you are guarding a good one-on-one player on the perimeter, do not fall for the first fake. Instead, take a half cheat-step backwards before reacting left or right. This momentary small retreat prevents being embarrassed by lateral deception and allows you to react to his/her real intention.

TWITTER WISDOM: "Sometimes it's more important to know what is not important." - @sportsmotto

APRIL 8

BIRTHDAY: Dario Saric 94, Terry Porter 63, Jimmy Walker 44, *John Havlicek 40

REBOUNDING GUARDS

Alert small guards can often be credited with multiple rebounds by being in the right place. With the preponderance of deep three point shots, there are more long rebounds that careen out into the key and wings. These rebounds can be gobbled up by aggressive guards who react quickly. Guards must also react to rebounds deflected off the hands of battling big men. Hustling to capture a 50-50 rebound deflection is as valuable as an above-the-rim thunderclap rebound.

TWITTER WISDOM: "It is not all about talent. It's about dependability, consistency, being coachable, and understanding what you need to do to improve." – Bill Belichick

APRIL 9

BIRTHDAY: Allen Crabbe 92, Kyle Macy 57, *Paul Arizin 28

SAYING NO

Learn to say "NO." This small word can have a big effect on your life. Nobody likes to deny requests or invitations and possibly hurt someone's feelings, but learning to say "NO" in a quick and tactful way protects your time as well as your priorities. You've got to consider whether trying to avoid hurting someone's feelings outweighs resenting yourself for doing something you don't want to do. As you get older, commitments and responsibilities increase dramatically. It is easy to get overwhelmed. Developing the habit and art of politely saying "NO" at appropriate times is both healthy and liberating.

TWITTER WISDOM: "It is a kindness to immediately refuse what you intend to deny." Publius Syrus

APRIL 10

BIRTHDAY: Nerlens Noel 94, Terry Teagle 60

KINDRED SPIRITS

Consider yourself extremely lucky if there is someone near your age who shares your vision and basketball dreams. Having a friend or teammate 'put in the work' alongside of you intensifies the effort and the reward. All of the individual drills become more competitive and the shooting drills can be more productive when each player shares rebounding responsibilities. More importantly, having someone witness and confirm your progress provides inspiration. Seeking basketball greatness does not have to be a lonely journey. A kindred spirit understands your secret desires and compulsion to pursue excellence and is riding shot-gun with you down glory road.

TWITTER WISDOM: When You Lose – I Lose!
When You Fight – I Fight!
When You Win – I Win! @SportsMotto

APRIL 11

BIRTHDAY: Janeth Arcain 69, Micheal Ray Richardson 55,

LITTLE MAN STRIP

Occasionally, an undersized guard finds himself under the basket with the giants. Rebounders are unaccustomed to a little guard circling under them. Invariably, the rebounder pulls the ball in a downward motion as he is landing. A guard who is alertly positioned can sweep upward with his hand as the rebounder and ball are coming down. The result is an easy steal. The coyote outwits the grizzly.

TWITTER WISDOM: "Confidence is quiet. Insecurity is loud." - Kari Bishop Goodwin

APRIL 12

DO ONE MORE THAN REQUESTED

One more push-up, one more chin-up, one more sit-up, one more weight rep, one more free throw than the coach or trainer requested. Attaching this small discipline to your mind-set separates you from the crowd of "wanna-be's." Refuse to be ordinary.

TWITTER WISDOM: "You have to be obsessed with the game in order to be a great player." – J.J. Watt

APRIL 13

BIRTHDAY: Tony Wroten 93, Quentin Richardson 80, Baron Davis 79, Dana Barros 67, Marvin "The Human Eraser" Webster 52

OUTLET PASS

Great fast breaks start with a great outlet pass. Rebounders who quickly locate a teammate on the wing or farther down court ignite the break. The most efficient rebounders can partially turn in the air to locate open guards awaiting the outlet. A strong, two-handed, above-the-head fling that leads the receiver down court triggers the momentum for the break. Guards can also help by performing two quick hand-claps to identify their location to the rebounder. Some alert stronger players can heave the ball down the court to a player who is open on a run-out.

TWITTER WISDOM: Pushing and getting through the uncomfortable by yourself builds a PLAYER. Pushing someone else through the uncomfortable builds a TEAM. - Tom Crean

APRIL 14

BIRTHDAY: Mark Macon 69, Cynthia Cooper 63

CAGE THAT MENTAL DEMON

There is a quiet opponent inside your head that wants to see you fail. He goes by several names: DOUBT, FEAR, INSECURITY, UNWORTHINESS, SECOND-GUESSER and many others. Unfortunately, many young athletes allow the demon to sit on their right shoulder and whisper negative thoughts that are difficult to ignore. With time and experience, an athlete can build a cage to permanently lock away this demon. This demon is pure illusion. When he rattles his cage, just turn off the lights and leave the room.

TWITTER WISDOM: "It's not who you are that holds you back, it's who you think you're not." - Unknown author

APRIL 15

BIRTHDAY: Vickie Johnson 72, Michael Cooper 56, Walt Hazard 42

CHARACTER

Character is always under construction. Having the confidence to do what is right even when it is inconvenient or unpopular requires uncommon inner strength. An athlete shows character in hundreds of ways: rolling out of bed at 5:00 a.m. to run, swim, or pump weights; pushing himself in every drill no matter if a coach is watching or not, never stooping to dirty tactics to get an unfair advantage, never retaliating to trash talk, never cheating with performance enhancing drugs, and never uttering the following sentence, "I'm not making excuses, BUT . . . ." One builds character brick by brick. We are faced with hundreds of moral decisions each day. Should I recycle this water bottle? Should I spread this juicy gossip? Should I ask a friend what questions are on the test? Should I cut in line in the cafeteria? Should I hold the door for the person who seems too far away? Do I let my friends in free to the game by opening the back door to the gym? One's character will dictate one's choices in all matters of right and wrong. Under most circumstances competitive sports contributes to building character, but one thing that cannot be denied is that under all circumstances competitive sports REVEALS character.

TWITTER WISDOM: "What you DO speaks so loudly, I can't hear what you are SAYING." – Ralph Waldo Emerson

DAILY TOPICS BY CATEGORY

ATTITUDE

A true competitor 2/17
Be a sponge 12/18
Coachability vs. Teachability 12/23
Dreams 10/15
Encouragement and positivity 2/11
Failure 10/28
Getting Benched 12/4
Gratitude 10/21
My turn to shoot 11/30
Passion 12/26
Pride 4/6
Respect 11/6
Respect the game 4/2
The Disease of Me 3/25
The gamer 12/9
The power of smiling 3/3
When the air goes out of the ball 1/6

FUNDAMENTALS

Baby Hook 3/25
Befriend the rim 2/9
Boxing out 11/13
Close out mechanics 12/24
Deception and misdirection 11/23
Footwork 11/25
Getting Open on the Wing 10/17
Grooving your shot 12/5
Hand-off techniques 12/27
Jump Stop for Balance and Safety 1/27
Outlet Pass 4/13
Screening 11/27
Shooting form - One size does not fit all 10/23
Shot Blocking 11/3
Taking a charge 11/18
Tap-Ins 3/23
The Quick Lift 3/13
Use the board 1/8

COMMUNICATION

Body Language 1/25
Confronting a teammate 10/25
Contributing from the bench 11/19
Create scoring opportunities 12/20
Dealing with a dirty player 12/31
Eye contact 10/19
How to become your coach's favorite player 12/25
How to treat referees 11/17
Influencing a ref's call 11/22

Lightning Source UK Ltd.
Milton Keynes UK
UKHW010943060223
416537UK00002B/310